Robert T. Sicora

612-251-7766

robtsicora@gmail.com

BUILDING TRUST

How To Get It! How To Keep It!

Also by Hyler Bracey:

Managing from the Heart
(with Jack Rosenblum, Aubrey Sanford and Roy Trueblood)

Winning the Race for Value
(with Barry Sheehy and Rick Frazier)

Secrets of Making Dreams Come True

BUILDING TRUST

How To Get It! How To Keep It!

Hyler Bracey, Ph.D.

For John Jones —
you are my first and best teacher about trust.
You talk it, walk it and live it. You have
touched me deeply by being a model of a loving,
supportive, effective human being and friend.
Thank you for the extraordinary impact you
have had on my (and thousands of others)
personal and professional life.

Table of Contents

ACKNOWLEDGEMENTS

For over 25 years I have been surrounded by great teachers, especially my business partners in The Atlanta Consulting Group, Aubrey Sanford, Jack Rosenblum and Roy Trueblood. Without their help in learning practical lessons about trust, this book would not have happened. My beautiful wife, Cass Flagg, has helped me be a better practitioner of the principles discussed here. As I say in my speeches, "If you can practice it at home, it is a 'piece of cake' at work." Also, without her love, support and editorial help this book would not have been as clear nor as personable.

Lou Savary has taken garbled ramblings and, with his wordsmith ability, made some sense of them. John Hurkmans' loving support has freed me to focus on getting this book done. Without them, this book would not have been birthed.

Thanks to all of you for helping me live my life purpose – to inspire others to live joyful, healthy, productive, spiritual lives.

INTRODUCTION

This is *not* a book about the importance of trust. The literature landscape is littered with thousands of books, articles and newspaper columns about the importance of trust. These include theories of why trust is important, polls about the degrees of trust people today and yesterday have or don't have, the adverse consequences of low trust, and its dire effects on investors and the economy. I'm certain you know all about these things, and that's not the reason you bought a book called *BUILDING TRUST: How To Get It! How To Keep It!*

The reason you bought this book is because it's about *how* to build trust and maintain it. Very few of the available printed materials on trust are practical and helpful. Of the thousands of pieces of writing I have studied on the topic of trust, almost none of them say: Here's a step-by-step method for building trust – interpersonally and organizationally.

I kept looking for material that would tell me straight out: "This is what you need to do first. That is what you need to do next. This is what you may be doing that's not helpful—and why. This is what you may have believed about trust-building until now, and here is why that's a flawed belief and won't really produce trust in the long haul."

What you believe about the way to build trust and maintain it is really important, and I've discovered there's a lot of flawed theory about the subject floating around.

Experience Is The Best Teacher?

Dr. W. Edwards Deming, one of the greatest quality gurus of the 20th century, used to ask his classes to raise their hands if they agreed with the saying "Experience is the best teacher." Invariably, almost every hand went up. Then Deming would say, "Experience alone teaches nothing." The audience would be startled into silence.

Just think about it for a minute. If experience is the best teacher, why isn't everybody a great automobile driver? It's been researched and found that people, after driving on their own for five thousand miles, learn nothing new. They gain no really useful knowledge about how to improve their driving skills.

If experience is the best teacher, why is it that by the time people are well into their careers everyone isn't an expert?

Or, why do more than half of all first marriages fail? And just as many second and third marriages?

Why do most mothers and fathers feel inadequate as parents, even though they've had many years of parenting experience?

Well, it's for the following reason. Experience itself teaches nothing, as Deming said. It's only when you link experience to a theory that you can, in fact, generate knowledge.

If you base your conclusions in a certain area on flawed theory, you will generate false knowledge. On the other hand, if you work with a valid theory, you will generate what Deming called "profound knowledge." It is only when you add theory to accompanying experience that you gain knowledge. Thus, the formula:

EXPERIENCE + THEORY = KNOWLEDGE

THE SUN CIRCLES THE EARTH

For thousands of years, people held a theory that the earth was flat. Each day, they would experience the sun coming up and the sun going down. So, they concluded, falsely, that the sun circles the earth.

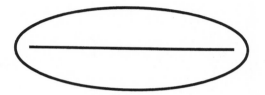

How many years of experience would it take to generate a different conclusion? It was only when new theories were proposed and tested did a new conclusion evolve that the sun is the center of our planetary system. By the way, in the beginning, hundreds of people were hung or burned at the stake for holding such a radical theory, and it took years to convince many. Even today, people talk about the sun coming up or the sun going down. So, proposing a new theory is not without risk, even if it is correct and leads to profound knowledge.

A lot of people still believe that experience itself is the teacher. But it's not. It's the theory that you hold and the experience that you apply to it that teaches and generates knowledge. For example, when the flawed theory about the relation of the sun to the earth was corrected, it really upset a lot of people, but in the long run it generated much profound knowledge.

The point is that neither experience alone nor theory

alone can generate valid knowledge. Profound knowledge comes with the right combination of both—**about anything.** The right combination of theory and experience is just as essential in trust-building as it is in discovering the orbits of celestial bodies.

Flawed Theory

What I want to do in this book is present some theories associated with trust that we have validated, and suggest some methods that have proven helpful in building trust. But first I want to focus on some flawed theories.

People hold many flawed beliefs or theories about trust-building that need to be dispelled. I hope to bring many of them to light throughout the book. For starters, here are a few popularly held theories about trust that, upon a moment's reflection, you will recognize as mistaken.

Flawed Theory #1. *"I hold an important title and a powerful position in this company so you should trust me."* A CEO might say, "I'm the CEO of this organization and therefore by the authority vested in me by the Board of Directors, I should be trusted to know best what is good for each employee. You should trust me without question or hesitation because of my position." Can you think of any CEOs fully vested with authority that you would not trust? The same case can be made for clergy, lawyers, teachers, parents, politicians, etc.

Flawed Theory #2. *"I have years of experience in this area so you should trust me."* Experience is often a necessary component if you want to build trust, but it is not sufficient to make it happen. Sometimes people with the richest and deepest experience can be morally corrupt and therefore unworthy of trust. Trust can only be built through appropriate interaction over time.

Flawed Theory #3. *"I am considered an expert in this field so you should trust me."* Perhaps this is why we have so many different, sometimes radically conflicting, theories about how to lose weight, each one designed by an expert who possesses the highest medical and nutritional qualifications. Since you can't trust every last one of these experts, how do you choose which to trust?

Flawed Theory #4. *"It's up to the other person to build their trust in me. It's your job to learn to trust me."* Many leaders and managers assume that trust is a one-sided responsibility, but the responsibility is not on their side. "If an employee doesn't trust me, it's the employee's lack of trust, not mine." The simple clarification needed here is to realize that trust happens primarily *between* people. It takes not one person, but two to create mutual trust.

Flawed Theory #5. *"I can win the trust of others simply by calling for it."* This is the theory of trust-on-demand. It reflects the approach of the classic horse trader or used car salesman. "You'll have to trust me on this." "Trust me, this is a great car."

High trust cannot be built simply on power, position, experience, expertise or fiat. Much more goes into the theory—and reality—of a trusting relationship than any of these. As W. Edwards Deming frequently told his workshop participants, "It's not what you don't know that will kill you, but what you know that's not so."

Throughout this book I will make reference to a company I once owned, The Atlanta Consulting Group. For the record, I have sold the company and am retired, so this book is all about sharing knowledge I have gained over the years and is <u>not</u> an attempt to get your business.

> ## MY PAINFUL USE OF FLAWED THEORY
>
> By age 27 I had a wife, four kids, a Ph.D. in management, two businesses, was racing stock cars and teaching MBA students—and I was an awful manager. That's why I can speak about building interpersonal trust with such passion today. I had built my career as a manager based on just about all five of those flawed theories. In my dealings with employees I was hard and cold, kick-ass-take-names sort of guy. I flaunted my title, my power, my experience, my education, and my higher degrees. I wanted all my underlings to remember the name of Hyler Bracey and to trust my authority when I demanded it.
>
> Everything broke down when I discovered that behind my back to just about everyone in the company my name was not Hyler Bracey but "Highly Abrasive."
>
> That's when I decided to take a year off to find good managerial training and learn some people skills. I really wanted to have good relationships with the employees who worked for me. When the entire department has named you Highly Abrasive you realize that both your theory and practice about workplace relationships is simply wrong.
>
> That sabbatical year became a life-turning experience for me. I had two rude awakenings. First, the way we in America were training managers and executives was not giving them the right people skills, especially in dealing with tough situations in the workplace. The second rude awakening was that I didn't have those skills myself and I hadn't a clue where to get them. So, I came out of that

year with one question burning in my mind:

How do you create trusting, supportive, productive interpersonal relationships at work?

What I dreamed of doing was finding a way to change the interpersonal atmosphere in the workplace from one of mistrust, fear, cynicism, dirty competition and a sense of helplessness and powerlessness, to one filled with joy, enthusiasm, cooperation, shared power and mutual trust.

Back in the late 1970s and early 80s, my dream was just that. A dream. At that time, I could find little or nothing truly useful and practical in the organizational literature and only bits and pieces of what I wanted in psychological publications. I attended at least 150 training events in those early years and still found little of what I was looking for.

That's when I started The Atlanta Consulting Group. Since the techniques and skills we were seeking were not then to be found in the business world, we decided not to study executives and managers, but to look for high-performing people in organizations. From exploring the dynamics of the relationships these high performers had with their bosses we began to uncover what we needed.

One great discovery was that mutual trust was at the bottom of it all. With a team of trainers and researchers throughout the 1980s and 90s, I helped develop people-skills training around the topic of trust-building and teamwork. We discovered if you could build trust into a relationship, it served as the oil that allowed all the machinery to work. "And you'd better not be a quart low."

Trust and Transformation

Our company task was to come up with a practical approach to answer the question that came out of my sabbatical experience:

How do you create and maintain trusting, supportive and productive relationships in the workplace?

It was the era of the first high tide in the quality movement in the United States. Watching the failed efforts of company after company trying to implement quality methods in their organizations, we realized that without interpersonal trust and team spirit built on trust, any attempt to institute total quality methods and other change efforts was doomed to fail. People couldn't just insert "quality" or (you fill in the name of your change effort) into their existing system, like a disk into a computer, because quality methods, to succeed, presume an atmosphere of high trust and intense teamwork.

In most cases that necessary atmosphere was not present. Workers didn't trust these new quality ideas, because the words and actions of their managers and executives were self-contradictory. Command-and-control behavior that instilled fear in the ranks didn't match the pretty words promising respect and involvement of workers and a workplace atmosphere free from fear, punishment and judgment.

To this day, trust and teamwork remain prerequisites for any genuine transformation of an organization. Few organizations actually commit to the time, training and effort required for building trust among their people interpersonally and corporately.

Through 28 years of positively affecting the economic

results of major firms, we learned how to measurably increase trust.

Managers and executives desperately need a basic method for building trust in the workplace.

That's why I'm writing this book.

The Trust-Building Model

Defining Trust

With all the flawed theory about trust floating around the organizational world, it is important to agree on a clear definition of the word *trust*, or at least a shared understanding of the concept, the theory behind it, and the way in which it is experienced, especially in the workplace.

First of all, it's not an easy task to define such a fundamental human experience. Intuitively, you might know what trust is, even though you don't have the basic words to conceptualize it. Or, you might claim that you would know it when you felt it. The problem is that words like trust, hope, and caring are such basic experiences that our definitions usually confuse the matter more than help it. Yet, it's essential to try. Let's start with the dictionary.

Webster defines trust as *"firm reliance in the honesty, dependability, strength or character of someone."* For Webster, to trust someone is to place your faith or confidence in them. But the dictionary misses a few elements of trust that are most commonly called for and essential in the workplace.

For example, I have discovered that when employees place their trust in a manager, it is usually only in a very specific area. Would I say that I deeply trust most of the people in my office? Well, they are all honest, dependable, strong and of good character. I firmly rely on them. So each one deserves my trust according to Webster. Yet, I would not trust a single one of them to perform heart surgery on

1

me. In organizations, therefore, trust usually has to do with specific abilities—a point Webster misses—and these abilities are often limited to a certain few areas. I know enough *not* to trust my highly-qualified accountant to repair my automobile.

Here is one of my attempts at a more organizationally-oriented definition of trust:

Trust is my faith in your ability or word in some specific area.

The word "faith" here refers to a belief or a conviction. It is much stronger than a wish, a guess or a probability. It says "I believe that you are capable of doing what you say you can do and that you will actually do it if you say you will."

Another nuance I think Webster misses, especially regarding trust at work, is that honesty and good character require more than not telling lies. My grandmother was as honest and as upright as they come, yet she often had strong opinions and ideas regarding matters she knew very little about. I could trust her to tell me whether or not she was angry with me or proud of me, but I could not trust her character evaluations of others in our community. For instance, she once assured me one of the preachers in town was an upright and saintly man. I knew from my friend who did yard work for him that he had a lot of skeletons in his closet and was regularly stuffing more of them in. When building trust among people in the workplace, it's important not only that they are honest in what they say but also that they truly know what they're talking about. Trust needs to be built in specific areas of expertise and performance, not globally.

Here's another definition I came up with that takes a slightly different focus. It underlines the fact that there are different levels of trust:

Trust includes the degree to which I believe you will look out for my best interests in a specific area.

This definition suggests that, like mercury in a thermometer, trust can rise or fall depending on the person and the situation. For example, it implies that I can trust some people more than others. It also allows that I can come to trust you more than I do now, or that I can lose some of my trust in you.

This definition also introduces the idea that part of a trusting relationship goes beyond believing you are capable and true to your word. It also suggests that you care about my welfare and success in helping me achieve my goals. Many people I know would clearly qualify as honest, dependable, strong and of good character (Webster's grounds for trust). Yet I don't believe for a moment that I can trust that they are looking out for my better interests. They might not stand in the way of my success in life, but I certainly can't count on them being in my service and advocating for my career. Any high-level trusting relationship in the workplace between a manager and a worker calls for this kind of advocacy.

My two definitions of trust cover situations that are one-sided, that is to say, "I trust you." They do not necessarily describe the two-sided nature of trust, the kind of mutual trust that says, "I trust you, you trust me. There is trust between us that we are capable and true to our word in those areas where we work together." Obviously, mutual trust is more desirable than one-sided trust.

In the end, I recognized that though trust was a basic and essential component in successful organizational life, it was a "loaded" word, tricky to define. Nevertheless, I realized I could propose a few important theories that are necessary and sufficient to achieve interpersonal trust among people in an organization.

* *Trust is never given to another person globally and unconditionally. It always has to do with a specific area of expertise or action.*
* *Trust involves both ability and word. You are capable in this area and true to your word if you promise to do something in that area.*
* *Trust comes in different degrees or levels, even as it is always defined relative to some area of action or behavior.*
* *Though trust can be one-sided, it is best when it is mutual.*
* *Trust can grow between people, or it can erode.*
* *Lost trust can also be recovered and rehabilitated.*
* *Trust can be built. There are methods and skills for facilitating it.*

BUILDING TRUST IN ACTION

Let me give you a simple example of how I attempt to build trust with a stranger. In retirement I have discovered a passion for speaking, so I often receive phone calls from potential clients to discuss possible speaking engagements. When someone calls, the first thing I do is ask why he or she called me. I want to find out what happened that caused him or her to seek me out specifically. This puts me in a listening mode and I can

---

begin to clarify the areas of expertise that are of concern to them.

Next, I find a way to show them that I am looking out for their best interests. I ask what they hope to accomplish at their meeting or presentation, and how I can best serve them. I listen to them talk. I find out what their needs are. I may replay in my own words what I hear them say to me, to verify that I am hearing their intentions and wishes clearly. I express my own reactions to what they say. I make myself as easily readable as possible over the phone, since they can't see my nonverbal responses. To do this, I may say things like, "I'm excited that you called." or "I like your ideas." or "I am concerned that approach will not work."

I invite them to spell out for me the goals of their meeting. I explain, "I need to know your desired results for the entire meeting if I am to help you achieve your purpose."

Sometimes I have to give my caller straight feedback. "It sounds like you don't have a clear aim for the meeting. Is there some person who owns responsibility for the success of the meeting that I should speak to?"

There are times when I decide not to accept the engagement. Perhaps my values don't match with the person sponsoring the meeting. I never agree to give talks that contradict or collide with my values. If I can't honestly be of service to the people who want to hire me, I am not going to become involved. I politely tell them that it probably won't work out for me because of the values conflict.

Building trust is not about selling myself or convincing people of my ideas and beliefs.

Once I agree to give a speech, I make a firm, specific,

time-bound agreement of something I am going to do that provides evidence that I keep my word. I may promise a speech outline, or a title and a summary, to be delivered to the client by a certain time and date ("by 5 PM, my time, on Friday"). I may also agree to call them at 10 AM the following day to give them my ideas for what I would present.

I make the call the next morning, not at five-before-ten or five-after-ten, but precisely at ten. If the client is on another line and not available to take my call, I ask the secretary to agree that "As soon as your boss is off the phone, will you tell him that I kept my ten o'clock appointment?" I do not hang up until I get this agreement or some appropriate one that ensures the client knows that I keep my word.

The Five-Step Model

The word TRUST has five letters in it and my trust-building model contains five elements. By luck and a bit of poetic license, each of the five elements begins with one of the letters of the word trust.

T means **be TRANSPARENT**
R means **be RESPONSIVE**
U means **USE CARING**
S means **be SINCERE**
T means **be TRUSTWORTHY**

I will spend a chapter developing each of these skills and sharing how they contribute to building and maintaining interpersonal trust. Here is a quick summary.

- To be *transparent* means to be open, easily readable and vulnerable. What you see is what you get.
- To be *responsive* means to give honest feedback respectfully, spontaneously and nonjudgmentally.
- To *use caring* means that whatever I say or do comes from my heart, so that my behavior is compassionate, affirming and understanding.
- To be *sincere* means to be congruent, integral, accountable, and keeping my actions consistent with my words.
- To be *trustworthy* means to be honest, to honor my word, and to manage by agreements.

If you review the previous example in the box, you will see that in my dealings with the client I used each of the five elements of my trust-building model.

Two Preliminary Questions

In an organization, you will not want, need, nor be expected to develop a trusting relationship with every person in the company. Therefore, two questions become key to deciding where you will expend energy on building trust.

The *first question* you want to ask when a relationship is suggested, offered or proposed is this:

Do I need or want a trusting relationship with this person?

If the answer is "no," then you are better off spending your trust-building efforts on relationships you do need or want.

However, there are times when I may not necessarily *want* a trusting relationship but *need* one. There may be a person at work whom I dislike for some reason, but with whom I am required to work or cooperate— perhaps I have been assigned to collaborate with this person on a certain project. While I may not *want* to develop a trust-based working relationship, I have a commitment to the aims of the company and I will *need* to develop a trust bond, precisely in the specific area of the project. Our trust bond may not extend beyond that specific area, and that's okay. (In the home, it may not be appropriate for married spouses to restrict their context of trust to one or two areas, but in the workplace such restriction is often most appropriate.)

CHOOSING NOT TO BUILD TRUST

I recently had a phone call from a man who attended one of my speeches. He said he was writing a book on trust and wanted us to collaborate and produce one book with shared authorship. For a number of reasons that immediately surfaced in my mind, I decided that I did not want to make any agreements with him about collaborating. I had nothing against the man. If I had agreed to write my book with him, I would have needed to build a trusting relationship. Since we were not going to collaborate, I did not *need* the relationship. Any involvement with him could bring entanglements about our respective book projects; therefore, I did not *want* a relationship with him either.

After I have answered in the affirmative to the question: *Do I need or want a trusting relationship with this person?*, I need to ask a *second question*:

Can I handle the worst consequences of this relationship?

Regarding the man at work that I don't personally like, the second question is very important to consider. Since I was impelled by my job to say "yes" to the first question, I need to consider if I can deal with the worst negative consequences or the best possible ones.

On the negative side, he and I could end up really hating one another. I could develop a lot of stress working with him. His values may collide with mine, putting us at cross-purposes. The project may continue on beyond the current schedule. And so on. If I decide I can handle these worst outcomes, I work to build the trust relationship.

If I want or need the relationship yet cannot handle its realistic negative consequences, I typically look for a "political" solution. For example, I may directly ask to be removed from the team, or I may suggest the name of another person to replace me. If my superiors insist that I work with this man, I may ask that a third person be assigned to the team as an intermediary between us to resolve the inevitable conflicts that will arise. These are some of what I call "political" solutions.

If, in my present job, I am frequently put into situations where I find it difficult to build trust with coworkers, I either need to change myself or change jobs.

My point is that, before you begin to devote the effort and time required to build a high trust relationship, it is wise to seriously ponder these two questions.

CONSEQUENCES TOO HEAVY

In the case of the man who wanted to collaborate on a book with me, I clearly said "no" to the first question, so the second question is moot. However, let's suppose that I did agree to co-author a book with him—or told him I would at least consider saying "yes" to the agreement. Then, I would have had to ponder this second question: *What would be the worst outcome, and could I handle it?*

The negative outcomes were quite evident to me. The man could be a procrastinator and our book might never get written. He might be a jealous person and would want more credit than his rightful share. If I spent time and effort to build a friendly relationship with him without collaborating with him, he might sue me when my book came out, claiming that I had stolen his ideas. These are some of the negative consequences that would have forced me to reject the relationship at the second question.

The following chapters explore the skills and actions in each of the TRUST areas. A final chapter on building trust at the organization level is included for clarification and contrast. Organizational trust is built on the foundation of high trust between people internally.

Building interpersonal trust is the first step.

Be Transparent

The first letter in TRUST, T, stands for Transparent. You will need to be transparent if you want to build a trusting relationship with someone.

To be interpersonally transparent is like being a window. If someone looks in a window of your home, they can see what's inside the room. Like that window in your home, transparency has three key qualities. (1) It allows what's inside to be easily visible and readable. (2) It provides a strategic openness. That is, it allows you to see what's in a specific room or area of the house, but not all parts of the house. (3) It makes you rather vulnerable.

The Transparency skills to be learned include the same three qualities: being *easily readable*, being *open*, and being *vulnerable*.

TRANSPARENCY CAN BE SCARY

When it became clear the role transparency plays in building trust it scared me. For my entire life I had been trained to "keep my cards close to my chest" and to wear a "poker face." I was concerned people would take advantage of my being vulnerable. More flawed theory!!!

Easily Readable

When I am easily readable or visible, you can look at me and quickly decipher my emotional state. My verbal and nonverbal clues, including my facial expression, my posture, and the tone of my voice, are some of the signals that tell you whether I am confused, excited, or upset with you as well as what I am likely to do next.

If I am not easily readable—I may do this by putting on a poker face or even pasting on a false smile—you can't tell if I am confused, excited or upset with you. Since you don't know how I am feeling, you can't know how to predict what I might do. You become wary of me. If you are wary, you will not trust me.

Great persons in history, like Martin Luther King and President Eisenhower, had easily readable faces. People always knew where they stood with them. If these great persons were pleased with others, people knew it instantly. If they were displeased, people knew that too. With them, what you saw was what you got.

When I am easily readable, you don't have to guess how I feel or what I am going to do next. It's obvious.

Being easily readable is a prerequisite for building trust. So is openness. Being easily readable has more to do with what I'm feeling and my emotional state toward others. Openness has more to do with what I'm thinking and sharing or not sharing with them.

Strategic Openness

I have found a lot of confusion among managers about openness. The first thing to point out is that total openness is just as destructive as total closed-ness. That is why I describe this quality as *strategic* openness.

A trusting relationship at work does not have the same requirements as an intimate spousal relationship. Even among spouses, total openness may not always be the best approach in every area of life.

Strategic openness means I am open regarding those areas where I want others to trust me, but not necessarily in other areas that have little or nothing to do with the job. When I am providing such openness in the context of work and the issues of the job, others don't have to guess where I, their manager, stand with them. I openly talk about the work or the issues surrounding it. I do it spontaneously, so they don't have to ask a lot of questions about the situation.

If they happen to have a question, I simply answer it beginning with, "I'm glad you asked that question." I don't say things like, "That's none of your business." If it has to do with the job or project, I want them to put their energy into it. It is their business just as much as it is mine.

Some of the things I need to be open about are:

• *My honest response to what they want or ask for.*

• *What I need from them to make the project successful.*

• *My strengths and weaknesses in my ability to help them.*

TELLING IT LIKE IT IS

Recently I was asked to speak to families of employees in a baseball stadium. The 2,000 people included a lot of children. Give me a thousand executives or managers, no problem. I am not used to crafting my message to fit children. Besides, we had a million logistical and technical problems to solve since I would be speaking outdoors.

My colleague, John, came to me asking a lot of technical questions about logistics.

My response was: "John, I am over my head here. I will figure out the speech. I need you to handle all the logistics in a way people can see me on the Jumbo Tron

---

Chapter 2

> and hear me without echoes. I am awful with details and impatient to deal with all the audio-visual people. I need your support just to make this speech happen. I will be happy to answer any questions about the speech and show up for any rehearsals or voice tests you need."
>
> Thank goodness, John did a super job and was a major part of my getting a standing ovation.

In strategic openness, my goal as manager is to cover all the bases. Employees don't have to ask me any questions, and they don't have to guess what I expect of them. Even when I am discussing a project over the phone, it is important in building trust that the other person doesn't hang up the phone with questions still stirring in his or her mind.

Among traditional managers there is a shared "wisdom" that a manager, like a good poker player, should not show his hand, keep his cards close to his chest, and present an unreadable face to the other players.

However, the fallacy is quite clear. In a poker game, the other players are my opponents. They do not trust me and I do not trust them. If they win, I lose. So, in a poker game I use poker-player wisdom to win and get the others to lose. In an organization, the other players are not my opponents, they are my partners. I do not apply the win/lose rules here. I want both of us to win. I use a win/win strategy instead. That demands my openness.

Poker-player wisdom will not build trust in employees. Rather, it will generate only mistrust. My guess is that if I were to use poker strategy in managing my family, my children would probably never come to me openly sharing their feelings, telling me their worries and concerns, asking my advice. Neither would I be talking to them about my joys, worries, troubles and hopes. Such an approach would most likely produce mistrust of me among my children. They would view me as their opponent in a win/lose game.

In contrast, if I would like them to share their life with me, I must be open about my own life with them.

If you were to ask me how to begin building trust with your family, I would say: Share the same areas of concern in your life that you would like them to be open about with you. Topics like your struggle with money, difficult decisions you are dealing with, your concerns at work, the dreams you have for yourself and your children, how you love them and want to show your love for them, the things that excite you, what you consider fun in your life. If you don't know what your children's dreams are, it's probably because you don't model by sharing your dreams with them.

To use the poker player's approach at home or at work is to use flawed theory. A more valid theory is that *openness begets openness*. When you are open and honest with people, they normally don't take advantage of it. They admire it and, more often than not, will return the openness.

Another flawed theory regarding openness in trust-building is: I will be open only when I can trust you. In other words, "Once I really get to know you, then I'll open up."

A more reliable theory is: *Openness precedes trust*. Granted, openness in this theory is risk-taking. I may get hurt in the process. If I want to build trust and reap its benefits, the risk is certainly well worth it.

Chapter 2

If I persist in waiting for others to trust me first, I may have to wait a long time, because they are operating on generations of mistrust of their managers. It's almost hard-wired into the workers' brains. So, if a trusting relationship is going to happen, I, as manager, will have to be first to be open. I'll have to take the risk. I'll have to be the one who is first and most vulnerable.

THE POWER OF OPENNESS

Foxhole buddies developed a closeness unknown to all others. They were closer than friends, closer than brothers. Their relationship was different from that of lovers. Their trust in and knowledge of each other was total. They got to know each other's life stories, what they did before they came into the Army, what their parents, brothers, and sisters were like, their teachers, what they liked to eat and drink, what their capabilities were. Sometimes they hated one another; more often they loved one another in a way known only to combat veterans. Without thinking about it, they would share their last bite or last drink of water or a blanket—and they would die for one another.[1]

[1] Stephen E. Ambrose, *Citizen Soldiers: The U.S. Army from the Normandy Beaches to the Bulge to the Surrender of Germany, June 7, 1944 – May 7, 1945* (New York: Simon & Schuster, 1997), pp. 266.

Vulnerability

All of us have one thing in common. At one time, we were all children who depended on others for just about everything. Also, each of us learned to get our way. What were some of the power tactics you used as a child to get your way? Were you a pleaser, a pest, a clown, a bully, a biter, a whiner, a pouter, a scrapper, a door-slammer, or something else? Whatever tactic worked for us as children, we discovered it was a source of power over others to get our way. We developed the theory that counseled: *The way I take care of myself in conflict or when I can't get my way is by using power.*

Then we grew up and became sophisticated. We still wanted to get our way, but we quickly learned that it didn't help to bite people or slam doors. We still held on to that childhood theory about power being the way to get our way in a conflict. As grown-ups, we might slightly rephrase the same flawed theory: *In resolving conflict—or getting your way—always come from a place of power and force.*

How many of us have said to ourselves, "Wait till I get to be in that higher position, then I'll get my way" or "When I make enough money, then I'll get my way" or "When I get (fill in the blank), then I'll get my way."

Whenever I use power to manage others, what I usually get in return is a lot of resistance. That means I'll lead a hard life as a manager. I know what I'm talking about. I've been there and done the power thing. It never built an iota of trust in my employees.

THE TIGHT FIST EXPERIMENT

At some of my speeches, I often do a simple experiment with the audience. I ask them to stand up and face one other person. One agrees to be Person A, the other Person B.

Chapter 2

I tell each Person A, "Make a tight fist with your hand." Then I tell each Person B, "Get that fist open, and get it open now." Almost every Person B starts trying to pry Person A's fist open using all their physical power. After a few moments, when I notice that a few succeed in forcing their partner's fist open and most fail, I say, "Stop! Let's try this again."

I begin, "Please follow my instructions. Person A make a fist again. Person B, do not touch your partner physically. Rather, establish eye contact and politely ask, 'Would you please open your fist for me?'"

Guess what happens? Almost everyone responds positively to this simple request and opens their fist.

Then, we compare the two situations. In the first case, people report they applied force and they got resistance in return. They applied more force, and got more resistance. In the second case, people making the polite request made themselves vulnerable to the other. They didn't get resistance, they got cooperation. The other benefit is that, while in the first situation there was one winner and one loser, in the second situation both people won.

The way to take care of yourself and the other person is not through force but through vulnerability.

In fact, I notice that whenever I am getting resistance, it's a sign I am not making a request from a place of vulnerability or I am not hearing the other person's request. The use of power to get people to do things for me will almost always evoke resistance.

I'm even willing to go so far as to claim the following paradox as a sustainable theory: *Perfect vulnerability equals perfect protection.* Who would ever have thought that something easier and less stressful like vulnerability is so much more powerful than force?

Vulnerability reflects a specific kind of behavior and attitude in trust-building. It differs from both being easily readable and openness. Being easily readable is primarily about my *emotions and behavior*. Being open is primarily about my *thoughts and intentions*. Being vulnerable is about *the consequences to me* when you do not honor my request. In vulnerability, I need to learn to make requests in such a way that the employee knows what the adverse consequences are for me—as well as the positive ones—if they do not honor my request. I'm talking about adverse consequences that happen to me, not to the employee.

NO LIQUID REFRESHMENTS

On my 10th anniversary with my beautiful wife Cass we decided to raft the Grand Canyon. Was I excited about the trip! As we boarded the plane for our evening tourist flight to Arizona, I began to plan how I was going to enjoy a nice celebration aboard with an appropriate wine toast. After departing, as the refreshment cart came down the aisle I could hear angry voices. When it got closer, it became clear what the problem was— the aircraft had not been stocked with alcohol in tourist class.

Now, I could have gotten mad as many other passengers had done. Instead, when the flight attendant arrived at our seats, I said, "I am a lucky man to be married to this beautiful woman for 10 years today. We had planned a wonderful celebration on this flight with wine included. It would be a real gift if you could find a way to help us make that happen."

She responded, "Let me see want I can do." In a short while, she delivered a large bundle of towels to us and said, "Keep this to yourselves or I am in big trouble—and happy anniversary." Cass and I enjoyed our celebration with two bottles of fine wine she had brought from first class.

I am using this vulnerability principle as I write this book. With all my strength I can't force a single person to buy this book, read it and put it into practice. From my position of vulnerability, I can say to you, "I have a dream of touching thousands of people with this book. I cannot succeed in teaching people how to build trusting relationships without your help. It would be a gift if you would say a good word about my book."

In that request, I have spelled out the adverse consequences for me if you do not honor my request. Namely, fewer people will discover this book and put its principles into practice. I will not realize my dream of touching others.

Summary

Transparency is the first quality you will need to begin building trusting relationships with your people.

First, *easily readable* behavior has to do primarily with showing my emotions. In transparency I make everything visible that needs to be visible in the specific area of our trusting relationship; nothing is hidden.

Flawed theory: Don't show your cards.

Healthy theory: What you see is what you get.

Second, *strategic openness* has to do primarily with my thoughts and intentions. There should be no need to ask questions because everything that you want or need to know I have made clear.

Flawed theory: I will open up to you only after I begin to trust you.

Healthy theory: Openness precedes trust.

Third, *vulnerability* has to do primarily with the practical consequences to me if you do not honor my request or trusting relationship. I have spelled out to others the positive and negative consequences to me if they do not honor my request.

Flawed theory: The best way to take care of myself is by using power and force.

Healthy theory: Perfect vulnerability leads to perfect protection.

Chapter 2

Be **R**esponsive

The second letter in TRUST, R, stands for Responsive. You will need to be responsive to others if you want to build a trusting relationship with them.

The primary behavior associated with responsiveness is giving and receiving feedback spontaneously, consciously and with care. The R skills to be learned include (1) how to welcome and respect honest feedback from others, as well as (2) how to offer the same to them. Learning both skills is essential in trust-building.

Giving Feedback

Giving feedback can be very helpful in building trust if it is delivered in the right way.

Historically in the workplace, the word feedback brings with it the expectation of criticism, evaluation, judgment and punishment. The traditional mandate to the manager giving feedback was to give brutally honest criticism. Unfortunately, managers who claimed to be brutally honest were usually more brutal than honest. Using feedback to pass judgment on a person reflects flawed theory. It can never provide a foundation for trusting relationships.

A more healthy theory about feedback's purpose, at least in the workplace, is: *The purpose of feedback is always to help build a trusting relationship in working toward a shared goal.*

In this theory, when a manager is giving feedback to an employee, the assumption is that the manager and employee

Chapter 3

are both committed to the success of the same goal, that they are not opponents but partners on the same team, and that they are both working for the same purpose. In this context, the mandate to the feedback-giver is to share your thoughts and feelings about what's happening in the area where we are trying to build trust in each other.

I define giving feedback as *my willingness and ability to respond to what you have said or done in a specific area, expressing thoughts and feelings that I personally own.*

A feedback sentence usually takes the form of "My reaction to X is Y," where X refers to what you have said or done in a specific area and Y refers to thoughts and feelings I personally own. My thoughts and feelings may be positive as well as negative. For example:

"When you didn't get the report in on time, I was disappointed."

"When you come home late and the dinner has gotten cold, I feel frustrated."

"It tickles me the clever way you are able to present your ideas in graphic form."

"The research you did on computers really pleased me for its thoroughness."

"On the last item you presented, I'm unclear. Could you flesh it out?"

In none of these cases did I make any judgments about the other person. I pointed to the words or behavior of the other person and expressed an emotional or conceptual reaction to those words or behaviors. My responses were about the behavior, and not aimed at the person. In other words, if some other person had said or done the same thing,

I would have responded in the same way. Healthy negative feedback is not given as a personal attack, nor should it be received as a personal attack.

Giving feedback goes well beyond casual conversation. Feedback has the clear purpose of promoting the success of the shared purpose and building trust in the relationship. A good football or basketball coach can give feedback that has the clear purpose, not of putting any person down, but of improving the team's performance, always in order to help the team play better.

Many companies have periodic programmed feedback meetings, sometimes referred to as Performance Appraisals or Performance Reviews. In these situations, the employee coming to see me is already tense, and may have been so for some hours or days in anticipation of getting negative feedback, something he or she may not want to hear. How do I give consequential feedback that builds trust instead of breaking it down?

Many areas of life sometimes call for negative feedback. Problems around money, salary, benefits, perks or wherever the person has an economic or financial stake in the outcome are often very touchy issues. Whenever something important is at risk or where adverse consequences seem evident around one's family, home, car, or job also sometimes require serious feedback. Difficulties with contracts and agreements, with new levels of relationship or with preservation of relationship can also test the skill of even an expert feedback-giver.

Fortunately, once you get used to giving feedback, including lots of positive feedback, you discover that much of the giving becomes spontaneous and easy. It's what I like to call "lightweight feedback."

In contrast, feedback where there is much more at stake and may or may not produce significant consequences I call "consequential feedback." This heavier feedback requires reflection and preparation, for to deliver it properly I must learn to tell the truth with compassion.

I have simplified giving consequential feedback into six distinct parts or a sequence of steps. It is essential that you learn this process and cover all the steps each time you give consequential feedback.

Step One: Knock on the Door.

If I am about to deliver consequential feedback, I'm probably tense and anxious to get it over with. To relieve my tension, I might like to storm through the person's door and hit him with it. But, who can know what's going on in the unsuspecting person's life at this moment. He may be on an important phone call. He may be finishing up a deadline. He may be ready to run out the door to an important meeting. For him, this may not be the best time to receive a message with significant consequences. He may be very distracted, and I may need his undivided attention for at least ten minutes to resolve the problem.

What I do, if I want to build or maintain trust with this person, is first "knock on the door" and say, "I have an important issue to talk over with you. Can we talk about it now? Is now a good time?"

This gives the other person a chance to say yes or no. He may say, "It's not a good time now, but can you tell me what it's about?"

Here is where I get a chance to be transparent. If the feedback is negative I might say something like,

"Jim, I'm upset about this morning's meeting. I need about ten minutes to discuss it with you. Is now a good time? I will need your undivided attention."

If my feedback message is positive, I would still do door-knocking.

"Molly, you did something on the project that I'm incredibly proud of and I want to talk to you about it. Are you in a place where you can fully hear what I have to say?"

What I am doing here is making it easy for Jim or Molly to say "no" or "later."

If they say "later," then I ask them to suggest a definite time to meet, a specific time when I can come back and give my feedback. I don't like to leave this first step without a firm and clear agreement about when I can return to give my feedback.

Step Two: Describe the Specific Action, Event or Behavior at Issue.

When I get together with Jim later, my first task is to describe the specific issue I want to focus upon. Generalized negative feedback is unrealistic and unfair. It's not possible that I can be upset with every single aspect of Jim's work on a project. But if there are two or three specific problems I have with his work, I deal with each one separately, proceeding through all the following steps with each issue.

"Jim, the issue I want to discuss with you is your arriving at the meeting today half an hour after it

was scheduled to begin."

Even when the feedback is positive, my first step is to announce the topic of the feedback.

"Molly, the issue I was so delighted about and what I want to address now is your presentation of the computer question."

Step Three: Spell Out Its Impact on You.

Next, I explain the emotional impact Jim's lateness had on me. I *do not* say something like, "Coming to a meeting late, Jim, is irresponsible behavior." Obviously I cannot know whether he was acting irresponsibly in the larger context, since I don't know the situation that accounted for his lateness. What I do know are my feelings when he was late, and that's what I say at this step.

"Jim, when you were late for the meeting this morning, I was embarrassed because I needed you there to make the presentation, and I wasn't prepared to do it myself."

"Molly, when you made the computer proposal at the meeting, I was incredibly impressed with how clear it was, how organized you were, and how few questions people needed to ask. You left nothing up in the air."

Most people giving feedback tend to stop after Step Three. But that's not enough. If I stop here, I assume that Jim or Molly will know what I want from them in the future. But how can they know? By not doing the following three steps, I am laying a burden on them of figuring out what is in my mind and what are my future expectations of them. This does not build trust. I have three more steps to complete before the feedback session is complete.

Step Four: Specify the Likely Positive and Negative Consequences and Make a Request.

If I desire a behavior change from Jim or Molly, or more of the same or perhaps something else, I can't expect the other person to be psychic. It's my job, not theirs, to figure out what result I want to come from this feedback meeting.

This step—specifying the "consequences"—is the only place in the feedback process where the other person can tell how serious I am about the matter, and the "request" is the only place in the process where the other person can find out what I would like to see happen in the future.

"Jim, if you show up late for another meeting, there will be consequences. Either I will simply cancel the meeting, I'll take you off the committee, or we won't deal with your agenda items—and for sure we're going to have this conversation again. I have a request of you. From now on, either show up on time or, if you're going to be late, give me early notice—at least one hour ahead."

"Molly, when you delivered your proposal on the computers, I was impressed with how you handled all the details and the way you organized everything. Anytime we're dealing with computer issues like this, I'm going to ask you to handle the presentations. I'd like you to use the same format. I have a request of you. I want you to take the same presentation you made for us and give it to the executive committee. It will certainly facilitate our next-year's budget request."

Step Five: Get a Firm Agreement.

In Step Four I made a specific request of each person, but I don't yet know that they will agree to it. So I need to ask for and secure their agreement.

"Jim, can I have an agreement that you will arrive at all future meetings on time or will notify me in plenty of time if you're going to be late? Would you be willing to agree to give me a one-hour notice if you are going to be late for a meeting?"

"Molly, would you be willing to get together with the President's secretary and be willing to make this presentation to the executive committee within the next month?"

If they cannot say "yes" to the agreement as I propose it, then I must negotiate an agreement to which they will say yes. I cannot leave the feedback session without an agreement for future behavior.

Most often, when people say "no" to my request, it is because they do not have the time, ability or access to the necessary resources to say "yes." So, I often need to ask—even when they have said "yes"—"Do you have the time, ability and all the necessary resources you need to complete my request?"

When I did not have a trusting relationship with my employees, in self-protection they would often say "yes" when they knew they did not have the time, ability or the necessary resources to fulfill my request. They said "yes" perhaps to make me feel good or to save face at the moment, hoping they would soon be able to figure out some way to wheedle out of my request.

Many people, even those with whom I enjoy a high level

of trust, are "pleasers," so I almost always ask if they honestly can say that they have the time, ability and resources to carry out the task. "If you don't have all three," I add, "perhaps we can find out how to get you what you need. If we can't, I will withdraw my request or we can negotiate a new request."

Step Six: Share Appreciation.

This step is necessary whenever the meeting has focused on negative feedback, but it is also usually welcome even after positive feedback.

The fact is that even when I give negative feedback, it refers to only a small element of the relationship. Nevertheless, the person may still wonder—but usually won't ask—whether everything else in the relationship is okay. Jim might be wondering, "Is he upset about more than my lateness? Is he happy with the rest of my performance?" Because people may be afraid of my answer, they don't ask. This is where showing appreciation comes in.

"Jim, I want you to know that when you are at meetings, you are always impeccably prepared, you are a good thinker, and you help move meetings forward productively. It's a real loss to the team when you're not there because you make such great contributions."

People need this kind of affirmation to keep the negative feedback in proper balance.

When managers don't share appreciation, employees who've been given negative feedback might do what I call a "dance" to test the waters of the relationship. They might drop by the office and ask the manager, "Want to get a cup of coffee?" or "Would you like to get a cup of coffee or a drink after work?" They are really asking, "Do you still respect, value and trust me?"

Receiving Feedback

How to receive feedback graciously and effectively is an essential part of building trust. When employees experience the fact that they are free to talk to me about anything and know they are not going to be punished or judged for it, the level of trust in our relationship will invariably go up.

When an employee wants to give me feedback, she might first test the waters. "Can I really tell my manager what I feel about where the project is headed?" or "Can I shoot straight with this guy?"

How much employees will trust me depends, in part, on my willingness and ability to solicit, sponsor, welcome and take in feedback from them, whether negative or positive.

Being willing to receive feedback is essential, but willingness doesn't of itself produce the ability to do it. Ability implies a skill one has developed. Learning the skill of receiving feedback is an essential part of building trust in the workplace.

Start from the fact that most employees have to build up their courage if they want to give a manager negative feedback. Some even have to generate angry feelings in order to bolster their courage.

If I need or want a trusting relationship with my employees, it is in my enlightened self-interest to be able to handle receiving feedback graciously, even if it is delivered in anger.

However, since most employees are not usually skilled in the six steps for giving feedback properly, I need to facilitate the other person through those six points to ensure that they do a good job of it. Even when they're furious.

Step One: Knock on the Door.

Some employees may not have the courage to initiate the feedback they desire to give me, but I can see that they very much want to. I can see that they may be disgruntled or shaking their head or giving some other nonverbal signal that all is not right. I don't have to wait around for them to take the initiative. I can simply ask for feedback. I can help them do Step One.

"Fred, I'm concerned that you're upset with me about something that happened at this morning's meeting, because you got real quiet while I was talking about the team's performance. Would this be a good time to talk about it?"

"Rebecca, I presented a new plan for computer installations in our office at the meeting this morning, and I was curious about your reaction to it. Would this be a good time to give me some honest feedback?"

"Milt, you seemed to be pleased with the way I handled that customer. Is that true? If it is, what specifically did you like about it? Would you like to talk to me about it now?"

"Alice, you and I just had a good sales call, but I'd be interested in your coaching, so that I might handle things even better next time. Do you have time now to spend a few minutes with me?"

Suppose an irate employee comes banging on my door and barging in my office when I am in the middle of an important phone call? I can still model Step One behavior.

"Lou, I can tell you're very upset. But right now I have an important conference call coming in. Can we set a time when we can get together? And I promise you in advance I will fully listen to you."

Then the two of us set a time for meeting at the earliest possible convenience. Allow at least 20 to 30 minutes for the scheduled encounter. Suggest a private space where neither party will be distracted or interrupted.

Step Two: Describe the Specific Action, Event or Behavior at Issue.

Although the expert feedback-giver would never judge, punish or put the other person down, I cannot expect that the employee will be so skilled. Although an expert feedback-giver would give very specific feedback and not say anything that was vague and too general, again, I cannot expect the employee will be so skilled.

I may begin by asking, "Can you be specific about what I did that upset you?"

In such a situation, I recommend what is called "active listening" in order to identify the specific event or behavior that's at issue. It may take some time, but this is a most critical step and should not be rushed.

The art of active listening involves the ability to let the employee express a thought, idea or feeling to me. I must listen to it attentively and carefully enough so that, when he or she has made a statement, I can paraphrase their position back to them.

"So you think it was dumb of me to talk to the officers about installing new computers in your department?"

The employee may say "yes" or he may go on to change, edit or clarify my paraphrase. When he does this, I again listen carefully and reflect in my own words what I heard him say.

"What you feel was out of place was for me to talk to the officers about the new computers before I spoke to the staff?"

Again, the employee may say "yes" or he may go on to change, edit or clarify my paraphrase.

I must continue to do active listening and paraphrasing the employee's position until the employee finally stops editing or clarifying what I say and indicates that I now understand his position.

Until the conversation reaches this point, I have not taken the employee completely through Step Two of the feedback process.

Most people receiving negative feedback, instead of listening carefully and paraphrasing the giver's feelings and thoughts, want to give excuses, blame others or deny that they did what they are accused of. "You have the facts wrong." "It wasn't me who suggested it." "It's part of my job to say that." "I was in a hurry and didn't have enough time to do it the right way." And so on. At this point in the process, excuses, blaming and denial are very *unhelpful*. So, I don't offer any.

If the employee did indeed get the facts incorrectly, I may offer to clarify them, *but only after I have done active listening and the employee tells me that I understand what he is feeling about the issue.* I might say, "I have some facts to the contrary," but I don't abort the feedback process by defending myself before I have heard him out.

Step Three: Spell Out Its Impact on You.

Here again, I may have to help the employee recognize and identify how my behavior impacted him and his staff. I might ask,

> *"What has happened with your group since I made the announcement about the new computers? What was the impact on you and them? What are they saying? What are they feeling?"*

I ask open-ended questions here to help the employee describe the reactions and responses that are happening in him and among his staff.

During this step I may discover ways to help the employee become aware of the need and appropriateness of making a request of me, which is the next step.

Step Four: Make a Request.

At this point, I solicit not a list of positive or negative consequences of my behavior, but I ask for the employee's (and his staff's) request.

> *"Now that you've felt heard and I understand your reactions to my behavior at the meeting, what is it you want of me? What is your request?"*

Sometimes the request is very simple. "I just wanted you to hear me out." Or, "I would like you to apologize."

If an apology is appropriate, I give it there and then.

Sometimes I may have to help the employee be specific about a request when it is too vague. A request like "Please

Chapter 3   36

don't do stuff like that anymore" is impossible to fulfill because it is over generalized and ambiguous.

I may ask him to be more specific, and he might do better but still not make his request quite clear or precise. For example, he might say, "Next time you're planning to talk to the officers, tell me first."

I may counter with,

"Well, I would be willing to agree to telling you first whenever it is an issue that directly concerns you and your staff. Is that a request you can be happy with?"

Usually, such clarification is helpful both to the employee and to me. After all, I do not want to agree to a request that I cannot in all honesty carry out, nor to a request I have not the time or ability to carry out.

Step Five: Get a Firm Agreement.

Usually, an employee doesn't realize the importance of this fifth step, so I usually introduce it directly. I might say,

"We need to get a firm agreement on this issue so it doesn't come up to upset you again."

When an employee makes a request, I have three options: Yes, No or Maybe.

First, ideally, the request is something I can readily agree to, so I can say "yes" to it. I normally am very clear that I am making it a firm agreement. I might say,

"Yes, you have my word that next time an issue comes up that directly concerns your staff, I will present it to you before I present it to the officers."

I might also say "no" to some request as it is voiced. For example, it may be outside of my power to make such an agreement, or company policy presently forbids me to carry out such a request, or the agreement requires the approval and/or cooperation of others. In such cases, I might say,

"I can't give you a firm agreement on that because such a decision also involves others and I can't speak for them. What I can agree to and give my word to is that when this issue arises again, I will ask for their support."

In other words, if I am going to make a firm agreement, I need to have the power and willingness to carry it out. Otherwise, the employee and I need to go back to the request step and negotiate a new request to which I can give my word.

Third, I can answer "maybe" to the request. It might take the form of,

"I can't make a promise to that agreement right now. Let me think about it. I do promise to give you a definite answer by noon today."

Never close a feedback session without some agreement about how you will behave in the future in a similar situation and then keeping your word. Keeping your word is essential in building and maintaining trust with your coworkers. If I don't keep my word, why should anyone trust me?

Step Six: Share Appreciation.

It is always important to end a feedback session by looking at the trusting relationship as a whole. Since the employee will normally not initiate this sixth step, I usually start it off with an open-ended question.

"Now that we have an agreement on the issue

you wanted to talk about, how are you and I doing in other areas? Is our relationship in general doing okay?"

If the employee doesn't offer more than a vague okay or is less than enthusiastic, I take it as a signal that there may be other issues that need to go through the six-step feedback process. So, I might go down a quick checklist of areas that affect the trust level of our relationship.

"How is the workload of your staff? Is it okay? Are they capable of dealing with it?"

If I get a positive comment in return, I might try another area like scheduling, work time, overtime. If those areas evoke a positive response, I might try others like health, people calling in sick, the spirit of the staff, adequacy of supplies and equipment, and so on.

When the employee hesitates over a certain topic, say, repair work not getting done, I ask a more specific question like, "Is that an issue that I can be helpful with?"

The close of a feedback session is a time for checking out how the rest of the relationship is going.

In general, by leading an employee approaching me with negative feedback through all the steps of the feedback process I not only don't lose his or her trust, I strengthen it.

Summary

In giving and receiving feedback responsively, I am trying to communicate a message of trust. I am in effect saying to them, "I am trying to build such trust between us that you can bring anything to me, even your anger and frustration with me, and I will treat it with respect and honor."

Flawed theory: Negative feedback and negative feelings erode trust between people.

Healthy theory: Giving and receiving negative feedback responsively can help remove roadblocks to trust and make it stronger than ever.

Flawed theory: Negative feedback is best when given short and swift.

Healthy theory: Negative feedback is best when taken through the full six steps of the process.

The six feedback steps are:

1. Knock on the Door.
2. Describe the Specific Action, Event or Behavior at Issue.
3. Spell Out Its Impact on You.
4. Specify the Likely Positive and Negative Consequences and Make a Request.
5. Get a Firm Agreement.
6. Share Appreciation.

Chapter 3

U se Caring

The third letter in TRUST, U, stands for Use Caring. You will need to learn the rather complex skill of showing care if you want to build and maintain trusting interpersonal relationships.

At first, I thought that the U in TRUST stood for Understanding. I have come to realize that understanding is only one part of caring, and that all the parts of caring are needed to maintain healthy trust.

If you recall, one of our early definitions of you trusting me included the belief that *I would look out for your best interests*. If that is part of what trust is about, what do I have to do for you to believe that I am looking out for your welfare?

You'd have to know that I care about you, and I care about our relationship.

We're not just talking here about that warm, soft kind of caring the way a mother might cuddle and coo a child to sleep as she spoke gentle words of love. We're talking about the kind of caring that, if I had an issue with you, you believe that I would come and talk to you about it in a way that you would know I care about you and our relationship. That's not soft caring but tough caring. It says that, no matter what negative criticism or strong emotion you bring to me, I will deal with it in a way that respects and protects you and our relationship.

In speeches, before I discuss caring as a key element in trust-building, I ask people in the audience, "Identify

Chapter 4

one person, besides your parents, who had a positive effect on you and whom you consider as an ideal leader, teacher, coach or boss." I ask them to clearly picture a scene with that person and "watch how they related to you, because that person has the qualities that you will need if you want to build strong, trusting, supportive and productive relationships with others."

You might want to try that same imaginative exercise yourself.

If you do, I'd be willing to bet that among the qualities of that ideal person, you would certainly list competent, confident and caring. If you want people to trust you and follow you, you must be a master of your craft (competent). Likewise, the healthy self-esteem you have about yourself (confident) influences your human actions more than anything else I know. People who are confident can influence others, make clear presentations and get heard, and are usually capable of being excellent listeners and problem-solvers in a meeting. Those with low self-esteem, who feel inadequate and weak, will tend to be defensive and argumentative in relationships.

Until the 1980s, the people on my consulting team and I considered only *competent* and *confident* as the essential leadership qualities. We discovered that while there were some competent and confident people we, as it were, would fall off a cliff for, there were others equally competent and confident that we would rather push off a cliff.

The reason we couldn't see the third quality of *caring* as essential was because we had bought into a flawed theory of leadership. We believed that *I have to be competent, confident, firm and tough to get people to follow me.*

We also held the flawed belief that *if I demonstrate caring to others, they will see me as weak and take advantage of me.*

What I now hold as healthy theory is: *Caring is a key component of interpersonal trust.* In fact, my caring for others is ultimately where my power lies.

Now, if you think back over the times you spent with your ideal leadership figure, I'll bet there were times when they got on your case, telling you things you did not want to hear. In your heart you knew they cared about you and valued their relationship with you.

Five Unspoken Requests

What does it take to show true caring? What can people do in the work setting to demonstrate caring? These were good questions, but we found we could not answer them, so we tried the reverse question. *When do people in the workplace—and elsewhere—feel cared for?*

This question turned out to be quite productive.

We discovered that people in the workplace have *five unspoken requests,* things they want but never ask for, don't even know how to ask for, and might even feel silly asking for. However, if you honor these five unspoken requests, people will know you care.

These five requests form the acronym HEART:

H stands for *"Hear and understand me."*

E stands for *"Even if you disagree, please don't make me wrong."*

A stands for *"Acknowledge the greatness within me."*

R stands for *"Remember to look for my loving intentions."*

T stands for *"Tell me the truth with compassion."*

WHEN ARE UNSPOKEN
REQUESTS PRESENT?

For a long time I wondered how to recognize these unspoken requests. What became clear was that anytime I am getting resistance from another person, one or more of the requests are present. Referring back to the "tight fist" exercise, when people symbolically start tightening their fist, I look for the request. As soon as I honor the request, as if by magic, our relationship will most often go from conflict to cooperative problem-solving.

My colleagues and I have developed these ideas more fully in a book called *Managing From The Heart*, that deals with the broader role of a manager. I will review them here as they relate to caring and trust-building in the workplace.

1. *"Hear and understand me."*

This is the first request that everyone in the workplace is silently making. They want me to listen and give evidence that I have heard *and* understood them deeply. We saw how important active listening was in giving and receiving feedback successfully. We use it again here to show caring.

Someone has called active listening a kind of "listening check." You can tell if I got your point if I can paraphrase your point back to you in my own words. In this way, I get your approval that you feel heard and understood. Once I assure you that you have been heard—I can tell this by your words or your nod of assent—I have made a listening check. In reflecting the person's statements, I don't have to paraphrase every single word, just what is pertinent to the issue.

Here's how I know the time to begin a listening check about something you've said:

- *Whenever you interrupt me.* (When you interrupt, I know that I'm missing something or I've got it wrong.)
- *Whenever you lose eye contact with me while I'm talking.* (Loss of eye contact tells me we are not together.)
- *Whenever you say to me, "Yes, but..."* (The "but" tells me I've missed something important and need to go back and bring it in.)
- *Whenever you repeat exactly what you said before.* (I missed what you said, so you say it again, hoping I'll get it this time.)
- *Whenever I notice strong emotions beginning to well up in you.* (I'd better make sure I get this part of your thought correctly because it's important to you.)

At any of these signals, I would go into paraphrasing until the other person grows quiet because he or she has been heard and understood.

2. *"Even if you disagree, please don't make me wrong."*

This unspoken request asks,

"However little you may value what I have said, done or thought, please don't attack my personhood. My opinion or position on this issue may be wrong, but it doesn't mean there is something radically useless about me. The fact

Chapter 4

that I have ideas you disagree with doesn't mean that I, as a person, am incapable or incompetent, that I am unloving or unlovable, that I am neither responsible nor responsive, or that I have no value or worth to you. If you disagree with what I said, then focus on what I said, not on me."

LEARNING A TOUGH LESSON

This was a tough lesson for me to learn as a manager and as a husband. My traditional way of preserving my self-esteem was to win every debate, to prevail in any disagreement, to come out on top in any confrontation. I won every argument with my ex-wife. I thought that the expression "win/win" with her meant that I had won twice!

Putting the other person down was my way of expressing my disagreement with any opinion you might have.

I am not proud of this but it taught me the price of making people wrong.

The reality is there are times when I may disagree with your opinion or idea, or I may disapprove of a way you have behaved. Yet I still want to show that I value you and our relationship. How do I do it without making you wrong as a person?

First, I have to "hear and understand you." I have to fully listen to you and paraphrase back to you your position or opinion to your satisfaction. In the process of doing this, I communicate to you that I care enough about your position that I take the time to fully understand it before I stand in judgment of it.

Second, when I respond, I must do so using "I-statements" about the position you took, not "You-statements." So, I begin my response,

"I feel confused about your position."

"I feel backed into a corner by your position."

"I feel strongly about another point of view. Let me explain it and my reasons for it."

"I'm concerned the approach you suggest won't work here."

"It seems you and I haven't explored all the alternatives yet."

If I were to begin with a You-statement it would turn out to be a judgment about you, and not about your position on the issue. Some typical You-statements might be,

"You are stupid to hold that position."

"You haven't learned to use your mind if you think that way."

"You don't really know how things work around here."

"You haven't taken the time to look at all the alternatives."

"You've got to be kidding! You can't be serious!"

Notice how even the subtler You-statements all have a little twist of the knife in them that infers "dummy" or "stupid." These are all making the person wrong, and not addressing the position itself.

After a speech to a large group of executives, I actually encountered an executive in the men's room who said he didn't understand that I/You-statement stuff. "I see no difference between them," he said. "I see no difference between saying, 'You're stupid' and 'I think you're stupid.'"

He did not realize that saying "I feel you're stupid" is just a You-statement in disguise. I learned I needed to do a better job of presenting the concept so people could grasp the difference between making an idea wrong and making a person wrong.

An I-statement can never be a judgment about the inherent worth of a person, because it is precisely about my emotional reaction to the content of the person's opinion.

3. "Acknowledge the greatness within me."

Yes, I mean *greatness*! In the United States, we confuse "being great," which is a quality of a few stars and famous people, with the fact that everyone possesses inherent greatness, uniqueness and value. By greatness I mean all those God-given talents, qualities and skills each person brings to the workplace and gives as a gift to a relationship and to the company. Every day, people are wishing you and I would acknowledge their greatness.

Unfortunately, we live in a culture where a person's liabilities and weaknesses are highlighted. In the classroom, we got homework and tests back full of red checkmarks. At home, children mostly hear comments like, "You're a bad boy," or "You're a naughty girl." or "How many times do I have to tell you to stop doing that?" or "You're always misbehaving." This pattern of emphasizing disapproval continues through life and has become habitual in the workplace. Workers hear from the boss or supervisor only when they've done something wrong or made a mistake.

Inside, every last human being is quietly begging, "If there is anything you admire or appreciate about me, I sure wish you would say something to me about it."

I'll give you two reasons why you and I should regularly acknowledge people's greatness.

The first is, *it's our job.* It's what you and I are paid to do as leaders, managers, parents or teachers. If we truly want to develop trusting, caring and productive relationships with other people, we have to acknowledge their greatness.

Ohio State University has been doing research since 1940 on the qualities that make companies, teams, groups, departments and families high-performing. Throughout almost 65 years of research, one variable consistently predicts high-performance: *In high-performing organizations, including family units, the ratio of positive feedback to negative feedback is 4 − 1.* What low-performing organizations score on this variable is often just the opposite, 4 pieces of negative feedback to 1 positive. Why is this put-down mentality so prevalent?

I think the flawed belief our culture promotes is: *The way to get people to do better on the job is to tell them what they are doing wrong and how to improve.* This belief breeds only discouragement and a loss of self-worth.

The healthier belief here is: *The way to get people to do better is to acknowledge what they are doing correctly.* With this positive approach, you are affirming successful behavior. Success breeds success.

Positive feedback is always welcomed. I have never known anyone who resents a compliment.

Specific positive feedback is far more powerful than generalized comments such as "Good work!" or "Nice job!" Rather, after the generalized comment, learn to attach three or four specific positive kudos. For example, after saying, "Great job!" I might add,

"I appreciate receiving this report ahead of time. I appreciate the way you put a short summary right up front. I'm glad you put all the complex research tables in the back. I like the way you put subheads in boldface throughout the report and underscored the ideas and facts you wanted not to be missed."

The second reason for me to consistently acknowledge people's greatness is that by doing it *I make a positive significant difference in a person's life.*

I feel very strongly about this.

I think people build up a kind of emotional reservoir around their sense of self-esteem to rely on in times of stress, weakness and failure. If that reservoir is filled with specific affirmations, they can call upon those reserves in difficult times. I know this personally.

A number of years ago, I suffered terrible burns that required skin grafts over 45% of my body, and I lost much of the agility in the use of my hands and fingers. Many people in my situation would have withdrawn from public life. I came back with more enthusiasm than ever and became a public speaker.

Seeing me resume my professional life with optimism and good spirits, people assumed it was my courage that made the difference and told me so. "What great courage you had!" they would say. I and people like me, who've come back from tragedy with renewed confidence, know it's not courage that made us survive. It's because they and I had been acknowledged and had developed an internal emotional reservoir of belief in ourselves.

LEARNING ABOUT OUR PERSONAL POWER

My burn accident required me to stay in the hospital for several months. Starting out with less than a 10% chance of living, my family and friends had a big celebration when I was released.

On the way out of the hospital the chief plastic surgeon leaned down and said, "Hyler, you know you are likely to turn into a hermit."

I looked at him and responded, "I don't know what you are talking about."

He asked "How many burned adults have you seen? None I bet. They are hiding."

That exchange really scared me.

On the way home, I had time to think about what he said and decided that I would not let fear stop me from doing anything I was scared to do because of my burns. Well, God kept upping the ante, and I was asked to do a speech to a thousand people in a distant city. I was very hesitant to do it since I looked so bad. I was still very much an invalid, but I said, "Yes, I'll be there."

Because I had little use of my hands and fingers, my wife literally dressed me and stuffed money in my coat pocket. Having the taxi driver fish money out of my pocket was a real adventure. That night in the hotel, I slept in my suit. I made the speech the next morning and received a big ovation. Personally, I was just relieved to be going home.

On the way home, I held a private conversation with myself. I concluded, "Enough is enough." I had slept in my suit and had not eaten for 36 hours.

It occurred to me people would say that what I did took courage. I knew it was not courage. As I reflected on what it was, it hit me. What had allowed me to do what I did was not courage. It was the people in my life, my Uncle Buddy, my parents, my grandmother, a share cropper Clyde Ginn, a school principal—all of them had acknowledged my greatness. I had been able to draw on that reservoir of positive feedback to do what I had done.

I realized the most powerful thing I could do was the same for others in my life. I could touch others by saying something positive, and they could keep that positive feeling in reserve and use it whenever they needed it. Every single person possesses that power. It is how YOU can make a difference in another person's life. You can touch thousands by how positively you treat them and affect how positively they are able to cope.

I ask you to start practicing giving specific affirmations to the people you relate to. Pay four times as much attention to what you admire and appreciate in people, then *say it to the person*. Build up their emotional reservoir, so that when difficult times come upon them they can cope, not only because they have courage, but because you have helped teach them to believe in themselves.

Since it takes thirty days to build a habit of giving specific positive affirmations, here's a trick that I learned when I was first developing that habit. Each morning, I put five Checkers pieces in my left-hand pocket. After I gave someone a specific positive affirmation, I would transfer one checker to my right-hand pocket. Soon, I began habitually to notice nice things to say, and I said them.

Another ground rule I made with myself then—and I still observe it—was that I could not leave any meeting until I had given at least one piece of positive feedback to each person in the room—publicly. These comments would take the form of an I-statement. For example, "I admire you when…" or "I really appreciated it when…" or "It was special to me when…" or "It was helpful to me when…"

4. *"Remember to look for my loving intentions."*

People usually have a positive reason for doing what they do. If what they do does not please us, we usually presume they have a negative or selfish reason for doing it. I wonder why? I think I have found at least one source of the problem. It's the difference between the *what* and the *how*.

The *what* of a project (or position, or proposal, etc.) refers to the object, aim or positive purpose of the project. It describes our intention, what we hope to see as the final result of the project. If I am committed to a project's purpose, then I am giving myself to it. My intention is not cold, but loving and maybe even passionate.

The *how* of a project refers to the method by which we want to get the *what* done. Here is where most of the arguments start. I think we ought to do it this way. You think we should do it that way. Of course, there must be a discussion about the *how.* The important caring point here is to acknowledge that we both want the same result or can support each other's commitment to the *what.*

I have discovered that, over 90 percent of the time, I can support an employee's purpose or intentions—the *what* he or she wants to accomplish. When we get involved in struggling over the *how,* I tend to forget the employee's loving intentions. I have learned that if I support their *what,* they are more often willing to explore alternative *hows.*

Suppose my office that does a lot of desktop publishing is about to invest in a new computer system? My office has traditionally used PCs, but one of the staff is very strong in proposing a shift to Apple computers. As I walk in, the discussion has grown quite heated, and the man arguing for the conversion to Apple has only a few people on his side. At the moment, he is really working hard to convince others to take his side.

To maintain the trusting relationship with him, I might begin by acknowledging his loving intention.

"Sam, I know your intention is to make our staff's work more efficient and effective. You want the best for all of us because you care about us and the desktop output we produce. You want whatever computer system we choose to be easy to use, have fewer crashes and be versatile in the layout of artwork. Isn't that right?"

By acknowledging Sam's loving intentions in the discussion, I have refocused the staff's unity in achieving the same *what*, and the need for their cooperation in finding a satisfactory *how*. I have also diffused their competitive stance and side-taking. I guarantee that at this point I could say to Sam,

"I want to support your loving purpose in this meeting. You have helped clarify for us the 'what' we want to achieve. I also want to support you in being willing to explore some other hows to achieve the what we all agree upon. Are you willing to do that? Are all of you willing to do that, since you all share the same care and concern for our office and the work we do?"

This distinction between the *what* and the *how* is central to resolving many disagreements.

Let's say I've been on the road for a while, and I've missed having some quality time with my wife. I suggest a *what*. "Let's have an evening out together where we are close and interact, a chance to reconnect deeply to one another." She eagerly agrees. We now have a shared loving intention. The *what* is clear. Then comes the deciding on a *how*. Shall it be dinner out, or a movie, or both? Shall it be something more active and interactive like dancing or bowling or miniature golf? To resolve the *how* decisions, especially if we disagree, we may have to reaffirm again and again our shared commitment to the *what*.

Many *how* discussions have to do with timing. We agree on the *what*, but we disagree on the *when* or *how soon*. The timing issue might revolve around having a neat desk. I, as manager, might like to have my desk top neat and clean at all times throughout the day. Others, however, while agreeing that neatness is desirable, prefer to interpret the neatness intention to mean that when they leave the office at the end of the day their desks are neat and clean. During the work hours of a busy day, however, having a neat and clean desk is not a priority.

In this case, I was caught up in the *when* and forgot the loving intention of my staff. Fortunately, one of them reminded me of their commitment to neatness—that we all shared the same loving intention—and asked me if we could discuss some alternative *hows* and *whens*, rather than an all-or-nothing solution. Thanks to that staffer, I was able to reorient myself. We came to some compromise agreement that all of us could live with happily.

Chapter 4

BEING TESTED AT HOME

It irritates Cass when I do not put things away. I call it our timing argument. I put things away, but sometimes about 12 hours later than her schedule would prefer.

Saturday afternoon, we had finished trimming the hedge. Since it was five o'clock, I decide to go pour us a glass of wine in preparation for our regular afternoon sharing time together. I was content that the tools would be put up the next day.

Then I heard the back door open accompanied by heavy footsteps. Something was up. She, in an irritated tone, said, "Hyler, can't you put the darn tools up?"

Now what I wanted to say was, "Get off my back. You know I hate yard work anyway." But I didn't. Instead I said, "Cass, I know your loving intention is for us to be completely through yard work today, so all we have to do tomorrow is hang out."

She responded, "Exactly."

I said, "Right now, I just want to be with you. You have my word that by nine in the morning all will be finished and we can just play the rest of the day."

Needless to say, that Saturday evening together was far better than it would have been the way I used to handle situations like that.

I am convinced if you can practice what is in this book at home, it becomes a "piece of cake" at work.

5. *"Tell me the truth with compassion."*

When I give speeches on *Managing From The Heart*, and go through the five silent requests that people make, I end with this one. I tell people that this is the final point I want to make and bet it is already in your consciousness.

Suppose you are my employee, and you have done something to irritate me. I have an issue with you about it. In this situation, I have three alternative behaviors from which to choose.

First, I can keep my irritation to myself. I could harbor my resentment, let it build up, and perhaps avoid coming into contact with you.

Second, I could talk about it behind your back. I could say to others, "Let me tell you what he did..."

Third, I could come and talk directly to you.

When I ask an audience which alternative they prefer, 100 percent choose the third one. Then, I ask them, "How many of you have ever personally used either the first or second approach?"

I get 100 percent of audience hands again.

"So, then," I ask them once more, "Which alternative are you telling everyone in this room you would like them to do in relation to you?"

They shout, "The third way."

So that's what I will do.

Because I want to maintain a trusting relationship with you, I am already committed to practicing the caring U of TRUST. I want to hear and understand you. I want to give you negative feedback without making you wrong. I want to acknowledge your greatness. I want to keep clear in my mind your loving intentions. Now, I need to tell you the truth with compassion.

This means that *I tell you the truth about what you have done in such a way that you have no doubt that I care about you and our relationship.*

This is a critical piece in building trust. If you want people to trust you, you need to honor this unspoken request always—to be told the truth with compassion.

Here's how I usually do it. Before I tell the other person the truth, I need to get three green lights, a green light in answer to each of the following questions.

First, *"Do I need or want this relationship?"* If I get a red light, meaning "no," I don't tell the person anything. If I get a green light, I proceed to the next question.

Second, *"Is my intention at this time to be helpful to this person and not to punish them?"* If I get a red light, I don't tell the person anything. If I get a green light, I proceed to the last question.

Third, *"Can I handle the worst realistic outcome of this confrontation?"* If I get a red light, then I don't confront. I do not want to take an inordinate risk of breaking the trust bond.

If I get three green lights, then I use the skills I have learned, especially those in the letter R of TRUST, in terms of giving negative feedback responsibly and responsively.

Summary

The third letter in TRUST is U and it calls for me to Use Caring in the way I deal with the other person. That person knows I truly care about them and their welfare when I recognize the five unspoken requests they make of me and honor those requests. Those unspoken requests can be summed up in the acronym HEART.

H asks: *"Hear and understand me."*

E asks: *"Even if you disagree, please don't make me wrong."*

A asks: *"Acknowledge the greatness within me."*

R asks: *"Remember to look for my loving intentions."*

T asks: *"Tell me the truth with compassion."*

In the past, people often couldn't recognize that *caring* was an essential quality of any leader because they had bought into a flawed theory of leadership. They said to themselves: *"I have to be competent, confident, firm and tough to get people to follow me."*

They also held the flawed belief: *"If I demonstrate caring to others, they will see me as weak and take advantage of me."*

We now know that healthy theory includes caring as a key component of interpersonal trust. "My caring for others is ultimately where my power lies."

Chapter 4

Be Sincere

The fourth letter in TRUST, S, stands for Sincere. To be sincere means to act without deceit or pretense. It is to be genuine and straightforward in relationships. It is to match my actions with my words.

Congruence

Another word I sometimes use to describe sincerity in a trusting relationship is *congruence*. To be congruent means that what goes on inside me matches what I say and do. In other words, my thoughts and feelings match my words and actions. If I am feeling grateful or relieved when a meeting I had been anxious about went well, I express that to the people I work with. If I am angry and frustrated about something, I find a caring way to communicate those feelings. If I have disagreements with others' thoughts or plans, I express my own thoughts and am open about my disagreement in a way that does not put others down. There can be no hype or hiding in my speech if I am sincere. I have nothing to fear from scrutiny or deeper inquiry.

If I want to build a trusting relationship, I will need to be sincere and congruent *consistently*. If I am congruent only now and then, others cannot put their trust in my word. Furthermore, such inconsistent behavior is confusing. When my words don't match my actions consistently, others don't know which way to turn. Will they choose to believe my words or will they choose to believe my actions in any specific situation? They know that one must be the truth and the other not. They can never know when to believe my words. For example, I can't verbally assert that I highly value integrity and then do things that are outside of integrity, such as cheating on an expense report, lying to workers about the company's competition, making promises I know I can't keep, announcing that "Quality is our top priority" and then measure people strictly based on their productivity and costs.

Another common example of a lack of sincerity often happens during a meeting. Suppose I have serious conflicting thoughts about the plans being made by the group, but pretend through silence that I agree with everyone else. Then, after the meeting, I privately express my disagreement to a few others. When my lack of congruence comes to light, people wonder when they can trust me to tell them the truth.

When people ask me, "How do you teach people to be sincere and congruent?" I confess that, of all the qualities surrounding trust, I don't know how to teach this. Qualities like sincerity and honesty are at the core of a person's values. They are core expressions of one's soul. I can't tell you how to make yourself be honest if you don't value honesty. In fact, if your values conflict with what has preceded in this book, you won't be able to build genuine trust with others in the long run. People will eventually find you out, as we have seen over and over in recent history.

I also do not know how to "teach" being congruent. Personally it took a lot of self-examination, therapy, growing and learning for me to unlearn a lot of advice I had assimilated in childhood. "Big boys don't cry." "Mature people don't show emotion." "Work is serious and hard." "Don't get mad, get even." How could I be congruent if I always behaved according to these beliefs? You, I hope, are far better off than I was. However, you may have picked up some commonly held bad habits.

Gossiping

Everyone has an innate curiosity about other people. We are all eager to get inside other people's beliefs, motivations, opinions—to know what they are thinking, saying, and doing, especially if the information is not common knowledge. As a result, we tend to like listening to gossip. Someone with gossip to tell can usually gain an audience, especially if he or she is a good storyteller and the information is "juicy."

The paradox is that gossipers "whisper" honesty and truth—"Let me tell you the honest truth about what Jim is doing when he gets back to his office. You may think he's doing this but he is really doing that." But the underlying message of the gossiper is, "I am not a person to be trusted with any confidential information."

The logical conclusion about one who gossips is that if he or she gossiped about so-and-so today, they may also gossip about me tomorrow. Therefore, I should not trust a gossip.

Nobody has ever proudly claimed to be a gossip.

We normally think of gossips as people who are low in the pecking order in an organization, but this is not altogether true. Managers and executives have been known to gossip. When they do, the harm they can wreck upon trusting relationships in the workplace is incalculable.

If I want to be a trusted person, I need to check to see if

Chapter 5

I am gossiping. It's a simple two-question check.

First, when I discuss with person B something person A has said or done, am I sure that person A would be comfortable with me saying it to person B?

Second, would I be comfortable going back to person A and telling them I had said this to person B?

If I can't say "yes" to both questions, then I am gossiping.

For example, if A had told me a fact in confidence, or had even hinted that this was confidential information, then I cannot even answer the first question with a yes.

Many people gossip habitually and/or unconsciously. They are not even aware that they do it, and might not even believe you if you told them they were gossiping. Perhaps their gossiping is subtly motivated because it makes them feel powerful or it gains the attention of others. Some may even believe that gossiping is a way to create intimacy— "We share something others do not know about."

Whatever the reason, if I want to build trust with others and I find myself gossiping, I need to become conscious of where and when I typically fall into my habit. Then, I need to stop myself whenever I notice myself ready to spill some secret or private fact to others for whom it is not intended. If I want or need a trusting relationship I must talk directly to the person, not about them.

Lying/Fibbing/Misleading

Lying is another practice that is contradictory to sincerity. Being untruthful about one's feelings or thoughts is ultimately incongruent behavior especially in those areas of the workplace where you want to build trust. For example, if someone asks me, "Are you upset with me and my performance on the project?" and I respond, "No, I'm not," when I really am, then I am lying.

Again, if the boss calls me on the carpet and I am angry because his criticism is misplaced, and I merely say "Thank you," and leave, I am lying. A trusting relationship at least requires a level of sincerity where I acknowledge my honest feelings.

The flawed theory here is the belief that *showing that I am tough and hard and can take it silently is the way to get ahead.*

A more healthy theory is: *When you have strong feelings about something important to the project, find a way to express those feelings with compassion. You will be respected for it.*

You might say, "I'm upset with your criticism and here's what the issue is."

Suppose I am resentful because I didn't get invited to a certain party. Instead of expressing my disappointment to someone who might be able to do something about it, I joke about the upcoming party and make sarcastic comments about it and some of the attendees. Perhaps, I am trying to hide my disappointment and falsely think that by disparaging the party I am gaining yardage.

Better to be sincere in your disappointment.

In my own professional life, becoming sincere and congruent took a long time and much psychotherapy. I wasn't a gossip, but I was unable to build trusting relationships for other reasons that reflected a lack of sincerity. I certainly never showed my feelings to my employees. I even denied having them to myself. I was more like the example of the person above who took his lumps stoically. When I was reprimanded, even unjustly, I would not confront but preferred to stew in my own anger and resentment.

Much of this behavior was so habitual that it operated beneath my conscious control, which is why I needed a professional counselor to help me recognize it and change my habits. I considered myself a person worthy of trust, yet I did many things to keep others from trusting me. We are indeed paradoxical creatures who seem ready to defeat ourselves at every turn. I shall always be grateful to my therapist for the "fair witness" he provided to my self-contradictory behavior.

LEARNING TO SHOW AFFECTION AS A REDNECK

Growing up I learned some interesting lessons about being macho and showing affection. To show affection toward males you learned three strategies—tease them, play tricks on them or borrow something.

In my development I became aware that these methods were not very sincere or direct. More sobering was my discovery that these behaviors affected how I expressed love and caring to my wife and children. During his lifetime, my Dad had only shaken my hand, never hugged or kissed me. So guess what? I never learned to show affection.

Over time I became more spontaneous and direct in showing emotions, including affection. When I learned it was okay to hug a man, I noticed I hugged my children more.

It is okay to say to someone, "I really care about you and treasure our relationship." If it is true, it is sincere.

It is okay to hug your in-laws and say, "I love you." It is okay to cry at a sad movie, a funeral, when a pet dies or when you are filled with joy. If the expression is real, it is congruent with your feelings.

Summary

To be sincere means to act without deceit or pretense. It is to be genuine and straightforward. It demands that I match my actions with my words.

Congruence is another word to describe this quality in a trusting relationship. To be congruent means that what goes on inside me matches what I say and do. In other words, my thoughts and feelings match my words and actions.

Common habits in the workplace that contradict sincerity are *gossiping, lying* and *hiding one's strong feelings,* especially when they relate to building trust in workplace relationships.

Chapter 5

Sincere ————————————————————

Be Trustworthy

The final letter in TRUST, T, stands for Trustworthy. Trustworthiness adds a certain quality to the S of Sincerity. Whereas sincerity requires your actions to be congruent with your words and thoughts, trustworthiness means you make your words mean something. If sincerity asks that you walk your talk, trustworthiness means you put your money where your mouth is. In other words, what you say is not only consistent with what you do, but trustworthiness means your words have consequences. Trustworthiness is about giving your word in an agreement and being willing to accept the consequences of that agreement.

Most people, I have found, treat their word rather loosely. For instance, because I want you to like me right now, I will say something right now that pleases you. I believe it serves me better to make you happy in the short run than to worry about the long run. My flawed theory is believing that if I say something right now that pleases you, it's of more value than telling the truth.

In the South, where I come from, we often tell people what they want to hear, rather than the truth, in the name of being socially polite. A typical exchange of acquaintances might go like this:

"Next time you're in town, why don't you stop by? Let's get together for a drink and dinner."

And I reply, "You bet! That's a great idea. Next time I'm in town I'll look you up."

The fact is, even though I like the fellow, my promise is

Chapter 6

not a true intention. I merely said "yes" to please him and get him to think well of me.

If I really had no serious intention to fulfill my promise, a more trustworthy reply to him would have been:

"Jack, I really enjoy our time together and personally treasure it. When I get to town on these visits I am really jammed and it's unlikely I'll be able to spend any time with you. I appreciate the invitation. Truly I do. It just would be unrealistic of me to make a promise that we would get together for an evening."

On the other hand, if I am hearing Jack's invitation as something seriously offered and I want to honor his request by meeting with him, a more trustworthy reply might be:

"Tell you what, Jack. If you're really serious about that offer of drinks and dinner, let's take a moment right now, get our calendars out and set a date and time. Otherwise, either you or I—or both of us—might forget our agreement."

Suppose someone in the office asks me to look into something for her and get right back to her. Well, "to get right back" may mean different things to each of us and to others. One person may interpret the phrase to mean, "I'll do it only if you call me back again." Or "I'll get it done within the week—or maybe the month." Or "I'll put it on my list of things to do. When I get around to it, it'll get done."

A more trustworthy response is to ask for clarification of what "get right back" means to the person asking. Only when she says, "By 'get right back' I mean within the hour," can you then decide whether or not you can enter into agreement with her request. You may not have the time at present because of some other pressing obligation. You may not have the resources or the required information to complete the task within the hour. You may need to get Frank's cooperation to complete the task and you do not at present know whether you can count on his availability.

I have found people habitually have become loose with their word by making:

- *Agreements out of politeness* – "We will call you next time we are in town."
- *Vague and ambiguous agreements* – "I'll look into that and get back with you."
- *Agreements they enter into with enthusiasm, forget and never bring up again* – I agree to be home by 6 PM. I arrive at 6:30 and hope my wife doesn't notice or mention it.
- *Agreements they don't intend to keep and hope the other person will forget* – Promising to take the kids camping next summer and hoping they will forget. If they mention it, I deny making such a promise.

How do I treat my word so that I'm considered trustworthy in the workplace as well as at home?

Honoring My Word

I haven't been able to come up with a more concise method or better set of rules for honoring my word than was used by a group of professionals called Right Management Consultants. They have a four-point process that fully supports the trust-building process. They call it "Working by Agreement."

```
┌─────────────────────────────────────────────────┐
│              WORKING BY AGREEMENT                 │
│  • Make only those agreements you intend to keep. │
│  • Avoid making or accepting "fuzzy" agreements.  │
│  • Give earliest notice when agreements must be broken. │
│  • Clean up broken agreements.                    │
└─────────────────────────────────────────────────┘
```

1. Make Only Agreements You Intend to Keep

This point means exactly what it says: I don't agree to anything I don't plan to carry out. I don't make promises I intend to forget. I don't belittle my word or use it loosely.

I like to divide agreements into those that are lightweight and those that are heavyweight. Lightweight agreements can usually be carried out with a modicum of effort and can be completed in a short time, such as making a phone call, setting up a meeting, carrying a report from one office to another, mailing a package, meeting for lunch, and so on. Heavyweight agreements usually require a good deal of effort, take a good deal of time, and can often have major consequences in the workplace, whether they are kept or broken.

We all know that people make a lot of agreements they don't intend to keep. How can you know when a proposed agreement is an agreement or when it is just a statement to please you?

Among lightweight agreements, one common sign of "pleasing" is when people use the word "try" in their agreements. "I'll try to get this to you later today." or "I'll try to set up a meeting with him soon."

The word "try" in an agreement often suggests "I'll get to it when I can." or "I'll do it if there's nothing else to do." or "I'll put a bit of effort into it, but it's not likely to get done."

Even with lightweight agreements, others may have a full expectation that I will do what I agreed to do. If I don't do it they conclude that I am not trustworthy. My failure to produce says to them that I don't follow through on my agreements. "If he is not trustworthy in smaller matters," they think, "how can he be trustworthy on weightier matters?"

Often during a speech I ask the audience, "Do you ever have people at work who tell you they're going to do something and then they don't do it?"

Every hand in the audience goes up.

Then I ask them to give me some adjectives they would use to describe such people who don't keep their agreements.

They shout out words like "Goof-off," "Untrustworthy," "Son of a so-and-so," "Snake," "Rat," and other epithets that are not printable here.

Then I ask the next question: "Have you yourself perhaps recently told someone you would do something and then never followed through or forgot about doing it?"

Most of the hands in the audience go up again, though a little more slowly than before.

"So," I say, "what adjectives do you think an audience might apply to you? Is this the reputation you want to have?"

I can watch the lights go on in their heads.

I never cease to be amazed that people who would condemn a certain behavior in another person are easily able to excuse themselves for acting in the very same way and believe that no one would ever condemn their doing it.

I am no exception to this paradoxical behavior.

Chapter 6

SHARING TOMATOES

Recently, a neighbor I ran into at the supermarket said to me, "I sure would like to have fresh tomatoes." So I replied, "Next time I pick some from my garden, I'll bring a bag over to your house for you and your wife to enjoy."

That was my Southern social politeness speaking. In my mind I made that promise to my neighbor. It was easy to do and I soon forgot it.

The flip side to this first point in Working by Agreement is, from time to time, you may have to refuse to make agreements because you cannot or have no intention of keeping them. The question is: How do you build trust when you have to say "no?"

When you must say no, you can at least reassure the other person that you value them and the relationship you have with them. To the person who invited you for a drink and dinner, you might say:

"Ken, I really care about you and I enjoy hanging out with you. When I'm in town on weekdays, I'm usually booked with business appointments. Our getting together will have to be on a weekend."

If I am not sure Ken's invitation is a serious offer, I may reply by putting the burden of the agreement on him, since he's the one who proposed the agreement.

"Ken, getting together sounds great to me, and I would enjoy hanging out with you. What I'd like for you to do is give me a call next Monday when I'm in my office looking at my calendar. We'll set up a time we can both agree on. Is that acceptable to you?"

> ## LOOKING FOR AN OPPORTUNITY TO BUILD TRUST
>
> When I am starting a new relationship I am proactive in building trust. One way of doing that is to make a firm agreement during our first interaction and keep it. For example, I might agree to send the person something (a book, article, picture, etc.) that day and call them the next day at a designated time we both agree will work (say, 2 PM). I Next-Day-Air the item to them, as promised, and call precisely at 1:59 PM. If I get an assistant, I tell them I have a telephone appointment at two. If the person is tied up, I get the assistant to agree to let them know I kept my agreed-upon telephone appointment.
>
> My experience has been that people are impressed with my impeccability in keeping agreements. Some have reported that they start acting with more integrity when they are dealing with me.

2. Avoid Making or Accepting "Fuzzy" Agreements

A fuzzy agreement is one whose words do not specify *what* is to be done, *how* it is to be done, or *when* it will be done. Thus, when I propose or shake hands on a fuzzy agreement, I cannot know when it will be done, how it will be done, and how I will know when it's accomplished.

Scores of fuzzy agreements are entered into in the workplace daily. A common example of a fuzzy agreement is when an employee says to me: "I'll look into that and get back with you."

I may assume the timing means "this week" but the employee may assume it means "this month." Such vague agreements make it easy for me to assume the employee has not kept his word because it didn't fit my expectations. Fuzzy agreements are set up to interfere with trust-building because they come with unspecific expectations.

Take the fuzziness out of any agreement you make in so far as possible. For example, instead of saying, "I'll look into that and get back with you," say, "I'll look into that question, get you a tentative answer by five o'clock today, and I'll have a typed up report with suggested recommendations on your desk by five tomorrow."

This latter statement has all the elements of a clear agreement. It tells the results I will produce, what time, how and where they will be delivered.

This recommendation also says not to *accept* fuzzy agreements. This means I will not let the other person propose a fuzzy agreement to me and have me agree to it. So, when the other person says to me, "Will you look into that and get back with me?" I might say in reply, "I can't agree to that. We need to propose a more specific date when you want the material."

The other might suggest, "Could you get me that completed file sometime next month?"

I might counter, "When would be the latest time next month acceptable to you?" When the other person is willing to settle for a fuzzy agreement, my job is to remove the fuzziness as much as possible, so that both of us can make an agreement we can both commit to.

The other might say, "The middle of the month would be great for me."

I still need to remove some fuzziness, so I say, "So, if I get the completed file to you on the 15th by five o'clock, is that okay?"

The other replies, "That will be perfect."

"So we now have a clear agreement," I say. "I'll get the file to you by the end of the workday on the 15th and you will be happy. Any questions?"

The point of this rule is that I make non-fuzzy agreements. Nor do I let anyone push me into a fuzzy agreement. I won't say "yes" to an agreement until the fuzziness is gone.

Now, sometimes it happens that in order to please me, an employee will promise the earliest possible date, expecting that I'm in a hurry and that's the promise I expect. He may be thinking, "Hyler is wondering when's the earliest possible moment I can get this done?"

In a case like this, when I sense an employee—or the auto repair shop manager, or my wife or my son—is giving an unrealistic time for completion, I may have to preamble my request before an agreement is made.

"Obviously, I want to get my car back soon, but I don't want you to make a promise you can't keep. Can we set a time when you feel sure my car will be done and I can absolutely count on its being done? I want to keep my life in order. I want you to be able to keep any agreement you make with me."

What happens if my boss asks for an agreement and it is not one I can keep? Suppose he says, "I need to have that report typed and on my desk by Friday morning."

Here, I need to report the impossible situation and negotiate an alternative date or an alternative solution to meet the boss's deadline. I might say,

"With what's on my plate right now, I can't realistically promise to get that report to you by

Chapter 6

Friday. You either need to help me figure out what other work I can put off my schedule, provide me with some extra help for the rest of the week, or extend your deadline."

Sometimes I am in control of all my assignments and can complete them without any outside help. At other times, to complete an assignment I may need the cooperation of another person, perhaps someone on my staff. In this case, I cannot make any agreement with my boss without contacting and obtaining an agreement with that other person.

If my boss and I are the only ones in the room at the time, I may make what I call a "lowest common denominator" agreement. I might say,

"I need the cooperation of my entire staff to complete what you're asking for, so I need to check with each of them about their availability to shift priorities. I can agree to let you know by e-mail by two o'clock if it's doable. If it's not, I'll suggest some alternatives."

The point here is that I cannot make agreements for other people. They need to be involved in the process.

When I am speaking, I often have people from the audience come up to me and ask if I would send them a copy of an article that I referred to in my speech. I usually say in reply, "Put your request on the back of your business card, and by (a specific time) I will mail it to you." Then, I add, for closure on the agreement, "If I don't have the article in my office, I agree to telephone you to let you know by Tuesday, so you won't be sitting around waiting for the article."

When I propose an agreement that's not going to work

for the other person, I have to listen and do problem-solving with them. Hopefully, we can problem solve together so that the situation can be a win-win for both of us.

I say, "When am I going to get that report you're working on?"

She says, "No earlier than two weeks from today."

I say, "That's unacceptable. I need that report for a board meeting scheduled for one o'clock Tuesday. What would it take for you to be willing and able to get it done before that meeting?"

This is when we start problem-solving together.

I should mention that sending a memo out stating when you want some job completed is not an agreement. It's more like an order. To have an agreement, the other person must say "yes" to your request.

When you are creating an agreement with a staff of fifteen people and you begin by stating the task to be completed, you need to ask the group collectively and individually,

"Will everyone agree and all give me your word that we will have this task completed and in the mail by Friday at five o'clock? Please raise your hand if you are willing to give me and the rest of the staff your word on this."

If some are not raising their hands, you might ask them individually, "What would it take for you to be willing and able to raise your hand and agree?"

As each person says what they would need before they commit to the task, discuss how to get it or do other forms of problem-solving. Agreement must be freely reached with each staff member.

3. Give Earliest Notice When an Agreement Will be Broken

There are many times when people make agreements and, for one reason or another, they get broken. The simplest case of this is when I have made a specific agreement that I fully intended to keep, but I see that it is not going to happen. It could be I had a flat tire driving to the office, my e-mail connection went down, someone failed to deliver a document they promised, etcetera.

Some people handle a situation like this by believing the flawed theory that:

$$No\ Results + An\ Excuse = Results$$

According to this theory, if I am late for a meeting *and* I have an excuse, it's the same as being on time. Or, instead of giving early notice that I'm going to be late with a report, I simply deliver the report late adding the reason why it was late. I expect the recipient will treat it as though the report was turned in on time.

I am stunned by how many people actually believe this formula to be realistic, and how many managers and executives hold it to be so.

In cases like this, what I didn't realize or appreciate is that this harms my trustworthiness because I did not keep my word. The persistence of this flawed theory and its consistent practice at home or at work must be attributable to some mass collusion.

A much more accurate formula is:

$$No\ Results + An\ Excuse = No\ Results + An\ Erosion\ of\ Trust$$

To protect my trustworthiness, *as soon as I perceive an agreement I have made is going to be broken, I (1) give immediate notice and (2) propose and negotiate a new agreement.*

Suppose I have a flat tire on my way to the office for an early meeting. I will do whatever it takes to get word to the other party. While talking to them I suggest that they either delay the meeting, put off my agenda items until I can get there, or cancel the meeting.

4. Clean Up Broken Agreements

Everyone of us has had the experience of making an agreement we fully intended to keep. Then we just forgot it. The time for the agreement to be fulfilled just passed, and it didn't happen. "I just blew it!" we might say.

Like most people in situations where they forgot about an agreement, I used to hope that the other people involved would be kind with me, not mention it, would quickly forget about it, would make light of it, or would provide their own excuses for my behavior. "No need to get upset, he's always late," I expect them to say.

When I break an agreement it is my responsibility to clean it up. The more serious the agreement or the more serious the result, the more effort I have to put into cleaning it up.

Usually the clean-up can take a very simple form.

"Folks, I'm half-an-hour late for this meeting thanks to a flat tire. I sincerely apologize for holding things up. You have my word that I will be on time in the future."

Or, to my wife:

"Two days ago you asked me to call Walt about the new insurance policy. I blew it. I forgot. I know you must be irritated because I gave you my word I would do it. I don't know what it would take for you to forgive me, so you must tell me. What would it take for me to get out of your doghouse?"

My effort to clean up a broken agreement shows I'm not nonchalant about my word. It also tells you that I want to reassure you that I care about you and our relationship, and that I want to be held as trustworthy by you in the future.

FINDING SOMEONE WITH INTEGRITY

Cass and I wanted to build a new home on our beautiful six acres in Atlanta but were leery of the experience. We had heard all the nightmare stories of building your own home. Cass, in charge of building the house, discovered the biggest problems were:

1. The builder not keeping agreements and consistently disappointing the homeowner.

2. The homeowner making changes during the building process and screwing up the builder's schedule.

She set out to find a builder who would keep agreements. With a number of builders, appointments for meetings were set up as well as dates by which specific documents would be mailed and dates for certain task completion. She paid attention to what happened.

One builder sent his wife to a meeting. Another arrived two hours late, with his excuses. A third came on time, but never sent the documents he agreed to send.

Finally, one builder, David Troughton, appeared on

time every time and sent us reports on time. We ultimately chose him to build the house. We were able to get a discount from his bid by making a firm agreement in writing that we would make no changes during construction, unless they were initiated by him. We had a great experience building that home.

Twenty years later David built us another home. Thank goodness, Cass knew how to verify the trustworthiness of builders.

Summary

The final T in TRUST is Trustworthiness, which goes one step beyond the S of Sincerity. While sincerity calls for congruence between my words and my actions, trustworthiness asks me to accept responsibility for the consequences of my words and actions. Trustworthiness asks me to be true to my word. Whenever I give my word that I will do something, I will do it.

Many people in the workplace and at home treat their "word" lightly and feel little compunction if they fail or forget to keep an agreement. Trustworthiness calls upon me to take my word seriously and to give my word only when I fully intend to keep a promise or an agreement.

It is difficult to build a trusting relationship with someone who does not live up to their word.

Flawed theory:

No Results + An Excuse = Results

Chapter 6

Healthy theory:

No Results + An Excuse = No Results + An Erosion of Trust

Four principles summarize the way to build and maintain trust in making agreements:
- *Make only those agreements you intend to keep.*
- *Avoid making or accepting "fuzzy" agreements.*
- *Give earliest notice when agreements must be broken.*
- *Clean up broken agreements.*

Managing Organizational Trust

Always Start With Interpersonal Trust

Organizational trust is built upon interpersonal trust. It is multi-layered. Some of the interpersonal layers that form the infrastructure of organizational trust include: trust between team members, trust between a supervisor and each of his or her employees, trust between cross-functional managers, and so on. If employees cannot trust managers and executives individually, they will not trust the corporation as a whole.

In an organization, trust works from the inside out. If it isn't happening one-to-one in the organization, it certainly can't be happening at the enterprise level. Interpersonal trust lies at the heart of all organizational trust.

Once again, this book is not discussing the importance of organizational trust. No one doubts or challenges that importance. Nor am I interested in replaying here the statistics that announce the continual erosion of trust in corporations. Many books, magazine articles and newspaper columns have already done enough to describe the angst and anger caused by such erosion. I am not interested in continuing the hand-wringing or those "Ain't it awful" conversations about the loss of trust in corporations. It's true and it is awful.

I'm interested in doing something about it. Something useful and practical.

As always, I am focused on ways to build trust. I am a how-to person. My practical aim in this chapter is to show higher-level managers and executives things they *can do* to build and maintain trust in their organization and *how to* do it.

It would require an entire book to do justice to the issue of managing trust at the organizational level. That is not the primary purpose of this book. But I do want to outline, for those interested, some of the essential elements I think go into the *how* of building healthy trust at the larger group level–the corporation, a department, a plant or store, or among members of a project team.

I want to outline strategy in three major areas: *long-term trust-building strategy, preventive medicine, and recovery from disaster*.

Long-Term Strategy for Building Organizational Trust

The first consideration is building and maintaining healthy trust within a group. From my research, experience and years of consulting around trust issues, I have isolated four critical components for building and maintaining healthy corporate trust, and they all need to be happening simultaneously. They are not sequential steps, but a system of components that interact together.

1. Provide Economic and Financial Education for All Employees. You need to provide your employees with economic and financial education about your organization. There must be an ongoing program to build and maintain financial and economic literacy among employees. Every employee must understand how the business works and be familiar with all of the major forces that impact the business.

If you don't do such education, employees are left to learn it through the random, biased and spotty information they may find in the media or through coffee-room gossip. If you want employees to act with economic responsibility and with financial accountability, they must have the information that enables them to act that way. For example, suppose no one has ever showed me, with a production sheet, how my being one day late with my quota of widgets can set the assembly line off by one day and cause the company to lose thousands or millions of dollars? I will go on thinking that the inexpensive brass widgets that I grind out in my little corner of the plant are inconsequential in the larger picture. How could I know how to be accountable?

Specifically, everyone in the company needs to know how to interpret a balance sheet, decipher an income statement, and follow the path of company cash flow. More importantly, they need to know how their particular area of responsibility affects the larger numbers and how their work fits into the larger picture.

For example, if I am a plant supervisor, I want the people who report to me to understand the market we're in as well as the market forces that influence us. I want them to be familiar with the economics of our plant, specifically the production numbers associated with our department. I want them to be literate about our organizational process and how our department makes a difference in the organizational scheme, that there are ways we could strengthen that process and ways we might cripple it.

MAKING ACCOUNTING FUN

When I was CEO of The Atlanta Consulting Group, our first attempts at making our employees financially literate about our company turned out to be boring to most

---

of them. We refused to give up. We felt it important in building trust, so we were challenged to make accounting fun. Fortunately, we found a one-day experience called The Accounting Game™ that turned out to be a most enjoyable way of making our people financially savvy. Last time I checked, it was still available from www.fla.provant.com/fla.asp.

A client of ours was a large processor of live chickens. While the chicken catchers and truck drivers had not been trained in accounting, they had been educated about the effect of missing the delivery schedule. They knew precisely what each minute of late delivery did to plant cost and efficiency. This was translated into its impact on the company's profit-sharing plan.

2. Develop a New Employee Paradigm. To build organizational trust these days, executives will most likely have to shift their organizational thinking toward a new employee paradigm. This may require changing certain corporate policies, systems, structures and practices.

In the old employee paradigm, employees might describe themselves like this: "If you hire me, I'll show up. I'll put up with all the red tape, bureaucracy and organizational silliness you lay on me in return for routine pay raises and the promise of long-term employment."

The old employee paradigm is dead and buried, or at least fractured and crushed. Most employees no longer see themselves in that outdated way. Recent turmoil in the economy, including layoffs reported daily in the media, has forced employees to see themselves in a new way. As a result, in order to build employee trust in the corporation employers and managers must learn to support the three things new employees want.

First, they want meaningful work. They want to be part of something bigger than just their job. They want to understand how what they do fits into the larger context of the organization. Fortunately, the Total Quality Movement and other employee involvement strategies have significantly contributed to achieving this first desire for meaningful work.

Second, they want an opportunity to impact decisions that affect them. Most employees are no longer willing to acquiesce to managerial whim regarding arbitrary decisions that affect them. They want to at least have the opportunity to influence those decisions. This does not mean that they demand to get their own way, but it does mean they want to be heard as part of the process.

My experience is that managers are often scared to ask for an employee's input because they believe that the result of "asking what the employee suggests and then not doing it" is worse than not asking at all. I think this is another example of flawed reasoning around trust. It shows a lack of valuing the employee.

So, if I am considering alternatives in the employee benefit package, I'd better at least do an informal survey to solicit the opinions of those who will be affected by the change.

In assisting organizations prior to my retirement, people on my consulting team normally showed managers how to solicit employee opinions ensuring that their ideas would be seriously considered but with no expectation that those ideas would be instituted.

Third, employees want good relationships at work. Historically, workers have tolerated having to take care of their needs for relationships and friendships somewhere off the job. Today, younger people especially are demanding collegial, collaborative and high-trust relationships in the workplace.

3. *Train Yourself and Others How to Build Interpersonal Trust.* As you know from reading this book, learning how to build interpersonal trust is not a simple or commonplace skill. People are not born as good relationship builders or good communicators. Relationship skills are not taught anywhere in our secondary school system. In fact, many of the beliefs ordinary people have been taught about building trust are flawed theories. As W. Edwards Deming frequently told his workshop participants, "It's not what you don't know that will kill you, but what you know that's not so." He's reminding us that when we can admit that we don't know the best practices to follow in building trust, we are less likely to go plunging into the deep without checking with those who know. On the other hand, when one is committed to a flawed theory, it can often take people exactly where they don't want to go.

It is also worth reminding ourselves that while this book may serve as a kind of road map to teach you how to find your way to healthy interpersonal trust, it does not drive you there. You have to develop the skills needed for driving and make the trip yourself. Nobody can do it for you. And to learn trust-building skills you don't already possess requires training.

Of the various trust-building training systems that I am aware of, I believe that a group called Right Management Consultants has the best available approach for teaching the kinds of skills necessary to implement what I have been discussing. I'm sure other groups may offer similar training. When considering different training groups for your company, evaluate and assess each training group against this model. For example, be sure the training gives your employees the opportunity to 1) practice the skills I've mentioned, 2) get feedback on their performance, and 3) a chance to experience the power of implementing the principles in this book.

4. *Create Structured Experiences for Building Interpersonal and Team Trust.* There was a time in my career when I used to assume that I had to get lucky and hope that trust among team members would naturally evolve over time. Sometimes I was lucky and it did. More often it didn't.

What I eventually discovered was that there are structured activities that can predictably facilitate trust-building, greatly accelerate the process and even improve it.

• At least once each year I would see to it that my team would hold an off-site two-day retreat-type meeting. I have found it helpful to have an outside facilitator design and manage that process.

• If I was named the new leader of a team, I would hold an off-site two-day meeting with the entire team in the 30-60 day window after my appointment. Again, I would have an outside facilitator design and manage the process.

• If I was the team leader and was given a new team member, I would insist that new member spend two hours in a structured meeting, with a printed agenda, one-on-one with each of the other team members as well as with me, the team leader.

• If I was new in a leadership or managerial job, I would strive to find a way, within 60 days, to get face-to-face with each individual employee responsible to me. I might choose to do this in groups in a seminar room or even in an auditorium, but it would be essential that I get in front of all my troops and look them in the eye. That means everyone who is below me in the hierarchy.

• If I discover I have two members on my team who have an unresolved personal conflict (typically originating outside the team agenda) and can't get over it themselves, I would insist they have a third-party outside-facilitator take them through their issues to the resolution of their conflict. Such negative emotional conflict, if left unresolved, will assuredly leak into the team's performance and infect it, thus interfering with any harmonious, productive teamwork. If the pair cannot resolve their conflict, I would suggest the two meet with the team leader who flips a coin. The one who wins the coin toss stays with the team, the other leaves. It's a purely chance operation, with no favoritism involved. I would lose credibility and trust if I simply tolerated having team members' emotions festering with interpersonal conflict.

Preventive Medicine

The first component, creating and maintaining corporate trust, is much like buying the right car. This second component is like doing regular preventive maintenance—changing oil, rotating tires, checking belts, restoring tire pressure, and so on. The question here is: What can you do to prevent the erosion or loss of trust in an organization to keep it from happening in the first place?

Humans have learned that it is better, whenever possible, to prevent sickness rather than have to cure it. The same is true with organizational trust. Better to keep up an active program of preventive maintenance than to have to suffer the losses incurred when recovery and rehabilitation are called for. Prevention of illness is much easier and far less costly than the fees of physicians, surgeons, hospitals and expensive medicines. The same is true for corporate trust. A penny of prevention is worth much more than a pound of cure.

As many CEOs and Boards of Directors have discovered, things like lying, cheating, cooking the books, keeping up a false front, and similar dishonest and illegal tactics don't really work in the long run as a satisfactory way of preventing the erosion of trust in an organization. What I suggest is a seven-point prevention system that can be used in any department, team or organization. It's all upright, honest and powerful.

1. Over-communicate. In organizations, people on first hearing seldom get the message of a change, a new policy, a new practice or a new process. In fact, researchers tell us that many employees don't fully get a message or trust it, especially an unwelcome or unpleasant one, until they have heard it at least six times in different ways. During these repetitions, it also helps to explain the reasons behind the new policy, how it will work, whom it will affect, etc. My wife is a careful shopper. If she is ordering something through the mail she typically doesn't make a purchase until she has received half a dozen catalogs from the company. So, employees typically don't "buy in" until they've heard the message half a dozen times. This principle is very important especially in areas where interpersonal or organizational trust is involved.

2. Show up in person. Overwhelmingly (over 80%), people tend to decide whether or not to believe a message by "reading" the nonverbal signals of the person who delivers the message. If you want to communicate something of importance that you want people to trust in and act upon, it's crucial that you show up in person to deliver the message the first time it is announced, even if you have to do it in an auditorium or elsewhere in front of a large group.

3. Don't be stingy with information. Avoid limiting the amount of facts you offer or trying to rigidly control the outflow of information. During times of change, particularly when trust in the corporation might be in question, people want to know a lot more than they need to know. So, let them know it. Be generous with information. Everyone involved needs to have available and to feel free to share as much information and opinions as possible about the proposed change. No employee question should go unanswered for more than 24 hours. In times of change, I also recommend having frequent short meetings to provide people with timely information that they want or are curious about, not merely what they need to know. Thus, three 15-minute "stand-up" meetings during a week are better than a one-hour meeting once.

For example, at every Ritz-Carlton hotel, cross-functional groups have stand-ups every day when they respond to two questions: *What did we learn from yesterday? What are we going to do today to create a special experience for our guests?* The cross-functional meeting is important because a waiter in the restaurant may overhear a customer staying on the tenth floor complain about the state of her bed linens. At the Ritz-Carlton, a housekeeper is always at that same meeting to hear the complaint and rectify it or see that someone in housekeeping rectifies it.

4. *Listen and empathize.* If you want to create an open high-trust organization, you can't afford to make people wrong, call them "bad" or put them down for having negative feelings about some policy, practice or situation in the organization. At one time or another, just about every employee for various reasons is bound to feel upset or frustrated with the company. If you want employees to be willing to be open about how things are going, you have to be willing to listen to them and empathize with their feelings, especially unpleasant ones. Remember, those negative emotions will not go away. They will instead go underground. Sadly, when this happens you will have lost an opportunity to solve a problem and to build trust. The key is to create structured ways for this to happen.

LEARNING FROM A CLIENT

Often, our clients turn out to be our best teachers. One of my favorite clients was always staying ahead of the competition by finding ways to deeply involve its workers in a program of continual improvement. One structure that worked well for them was the rotating "Open Department Meeting." At least once a year, employees in each department would be invited to a conference room to meet with major company executives, without their boss present. They could ask any question they had on their mind. They could also bring a question given to them by someone in another department, whose department would not be having an open meeting for

---

some months. (Everyone knew when these meeting were being held, so anyone with an issue could feed questions through a friend attending a meeting.)

Executives promised that all questions *with answers* would be posted throughout the company within 24 hours. Here are two Q&As that I have personally seen:

Question: Why can't we have tools at our workstations to do minor repairs?

Answer: There is no reason you cannot have the tools you need. Thank you for being willing to do minor repairs. Tool chests will be delivered to your stations Friday, and maintenance will inquire about any training you desire by the end of the month. If you do not have the tools you need by Friday 5 PM, call Clarence, our Senior VP of Manufacturing at extension 6628.

Question: Why is our supervisor Keith being so critical of our work this month? We can't seem to do anything right.

Answer: We do not know. By the time you read this, Keith has agreed to meet with you and assess what is going on. He also will post his responses next Monday with corrective action agreed to by all of you. If this is not handled to your satisfaction, please call Bill, our HR Director at extension 7722.

5. Confront denial. Suppose something bad or destructive to the organization or team spirit is going on among the staff. You discover that people are continuing with their work as if nothing was wrong. You don't say anything about it. Eventually the negative effects of that destructive behavior will appear for all to see, and there will be unwelcome consequences. People will resent the fact that you didn't call everyone's conscious attention to the problem. You will lose credibility in their eyes. You will lose the trust they had in you, because they expected you to be looking out for them and for the team. It's as if they say to you, "We were in denial. You should have said something to wake us up before the bad consequences happened. You didn't. You let it go on."

6. *Never say never.* In today's rapidly changing world, don't make promises you can't keep. Don't make agreements that are outside your control. "Is that the last of the layoffs?" someone may ask. You cannot say yes or no in reply if you're not in control of layoffs. To say yes or no, if outside of your control, can only weaken your trust relationship when some promise you made turns out to be the opposite of what happens.

7. *Be careful of your hiring and firing practices.* Employees watch carefully how you hire and fire people. Whom you hire and whom you fire or don't fire influences your credibility and trust among employees. Many managers underestimate the power of their behavior in this area. I can assure you that people on a team pay careful attention to what you will tolerate from a team member. For example, what is the lowest common denominator of job performance you are willing to accept?

If as a team leader you say you want high performance, yet you tolerate low performance from some, your word will receive little credibility and less trust on performance. If you say you want teamwork and team spirit, but you name as team members independent, free-spirited hip-shooters, you will have little credibility whenever you talk about teamwork.

To build performance and teamwork credibility and trust, I suggest you hold what I call "public celebrations" and "public hangings." Hire people who epitomize the qualities you want in the rest of the team in terms of values, skills, behavior and performance. When they are introduced to the team, have a celebration of their joining. Explain their qualities and how they will help the team be successful. You may then go around and introduce the others to the new member pointing out their special talents as you introduce them.

When you let someone go, gather the other team members behind closed doors and explain how the person being fired violated the expected team behaviors and values. At such a "hanging," also explain your personal reasons for making the dismissal.

Recovery and Rehabilitation

Recovery of your car from a major accident requires more than additional preventive maintenance. It requires specialized outside help. But don't look to me for this service, since I am retired from consulting and only do speaking. I mention this here explicitly because I am afraid some will discount what I am recommending thinking I am trying to drum up consulting jobs. As a birthday gift to my wife some years ago, I agreed to stop consulting.

What do you do in an organization when trust has been shipwrecked and the organization needs to recover from it? This too is a special case and requires specialized outside help, depending on the severity of the wreck.

To discuss this issue in depth is far beyond the scope of this book, and managers will need more than a glove-compartment owner's manual to perform the necessary repair and rehabilitation. But I will mention a few of the key components that need to be addressed.

• *Sponsor Grieving.* Create venues where people can express their negative feelings or sense of loss. The organization can never get beyond the wreckage stage until people have an organizational context for expressing the hurt, anger, betrayal, frustration and other strong emotions they may feel.

• *Multiply Appreciation.* When an organization is trying to recover from a destruction of trust or credibility, the employees still on the scene will be called upon to do much more work than usual, even though they may not feel like doing it. Since everyone must work much harder just to survive during these times of stress and strain, employees need to receive a tremendous amount of appreciation and affirmation. Such appreciation is usually left out. Employees putting out the extra effort feel underappreciated, while managers get so busy with details that they forget to lavish praise. Thus, the amount of appreciation goes down precisely when it needs to go up. This is when and where it is most needed.

• *Communicate, Communicate, Communicate.* During recovery, people become ravenous for information. In my more than thirty years of managing organizations and consulting to others, I have never had anyone say to me, "I'm getting too much information about what's happening here and how it affects me."

• *Eliminate Waste and Unnecessary Tasks.* As a manager during the tough times of recovery from an organizational trust wreck, you can build a lot of credibility by quickly eliminating any task that is superfluous, unnecessary or a waste of time. This shows you are on the workers' side. My suggestion to managers is to address your department or team and say:

"If you come across any task that is unnecessary or wasteful of our time that we could eliminate without reducing the quality or quantity of our performance, let's just eliminate it. Whatever it is, just go ahead and drop it, and we'll see if anybody notices or complains."

What then happens is most of the red tape and bureaucracy trivia gets left behind, workers are grateful, and everyone gets the important work done.

Summary

In this chapter I shared some of the essential elements that I think would go into building healthy trust at the department, plant and corporate levels.

I outlined strategy in three major areas: *long-term trust-building, preventive medicine, and recovery from disaster.*

In long-term trust building, I suggested four practices to be done simultaneously and continually:

* *Provide economic and financial education for all employees.*
* *Develop a new employee paradigm.*
* *Train yourself and others on how to build interpersonal trust.*
* *Create structured experiences for building interpersonal and team trust.*

Under preventive medicine, I suggested seven practices that would be useful to executives and managers for maintaining trust in times of change:

- *Over-communicate.*
- *Show up in person.*
- *Don't be stingy with information.*
- *Listen and empathize.*
- *Confront denial.*
- *Never say never.*
- *Be careful with your hiring and firing practices.*

Just as recovery of your car from a major accident requires more than additional preventive maintenance, the same goes for a corporate trust wreck. I suggested four extraordinary practices that might help restoration of trust:

- *Sponsor grieving.*
- *Multiply appreciation.*
- *Communicate, communicate, communicate.*
- *Eliminate waste and unnecessary tasks.*

It goes without saying that building and re-building trust in corporations is not a simple matter. Furthermore, when people's trust in one or two well-known corporations is shattered, they become suspicious of all other organizations. With public confidence shaken, it becomes even harder for organizations to maintain employee trust, investor trust, stakeholder trust and popular trust. In such situations, perhaps interpersonal trust—one-on-one trust-building—is the best that can be hoped for, which is why I focused this book on how trust can be achieved interpersonally.

Chapter 7

Made in the USA
San Bernardino, CA
07 August 2015